Getting Started With Micro Focus Personal COBOL™ 2.0

John B. Crawford
Cal Poly University, Pomona

Consulting Editors

Nancy Stern
Hofstra University

Robert A. Stern
Nassau Community College

John Wiley & Sons, Inc.
New York • Chichester • Brisbane • Toronto • Singapore

In recognition of the importance of preserving what has been written, it is a policy of John Wiley & Sons, Inc., to have books of enduring value published in the United States printed on acid-free paper, and we exert our best efforts to that end.

ISBN: 0-471-30680-0

Printed in the United States of America

10 9 8 7 6 5 4

Table of Contents

Chapter 4 Using the Personal COBOL Editor

Chapter 5 Compiling COBOL Programs

Chapter 6 Developing Test Data Files

Chapter 7 Program Testing with Animator

Chapter 8 Additional Features of Personal COBOL

Appendix A A Microcomputer Primer for Newcomers

Preface

The Micro Focus Personal COBOL System which accompanies this manual is a comprehensive package for use in developing computer programs in COBOL. The package consists of the Personal COBOL 2.0 software as well as the Personal COBOL 2.0 *Programmer's Guide*. The software includes an editor specifically designed to enter and modify COBOL programs. It also includes a COBOL compiler that fully supports the ANSI 85 COBOL standard. In addition, a testing and debugging tool called Animator is included which permits step-by-step execution and program monitoring. On-line help and sample programs are also included as part of the software. The software may be used on any personal computer that has DOS 3.3 or higher and a minimum of 640K of RAM, 3MB of hard disk space, and one 3.5" high density disk drive.

My purpose in writing this manual was to provide the beginning computer programming student with the minimum information necessary to get started with the Micro Focus Personal COBOL System. The manual provides explanations of how to install the system, how to enter and edit programs, and how to debug and test them. I recommend that students begin their introduction to the Personal COBOL software by first reading this manual and then using the *Programmer's Guide* as a reference and source of additional information.

This manual is not designed to teach COBOL. I assume this manual and the Micro Focus Personal COBOL System will be used in conjunction with a COBOL textbook designed to teach COBOL syntax and programming rules, such as *Structured COBOL Programming, 7th Edition,* by Nancy Stern and Robert A. Stern, also published in 1994 by John Wiley & Sons, Inc.

I have written this manual assuming that its readers have some experience using a personal computer and the DOS operating system. Those without this background may wish to begin by reading the appendix in this manual written by James Janossy. It explains fundamental concepts related to using these computing resources.

Thanks to the following reviewers who extended valuable feedback on the manuscript: John Plotnicki, Colorado State University; Emerson Maxson, Boise State University; William S. Remington, Middle Tennessee State University; Kenneth T. Fougere, Bryant College.

Dr. John B. Crawford
Professor
Computer Information Systems
Cal Poly University, Pomona

NOTE: You can obtain additional copies of this guide and the Micro Focus Personal COBOL system by contacting your local Wiley sales representative or by contacting MIS Marketing Manager, College Division, John Wiley & Sons, 605 Third Avenue, New York, NY 10158, (212) 850-6480.

If you have any questions about the material in this guide or would like to make any suggestions, you can do so by contacting MIS Editor, College Division, John Wiley & Sons, 605 Third Avenue, New York, NY 10158, (212) 850-8619.

To order additional copies of this guide outside the United States, please use the following addresses:

In Canada, write to: College Division, John Wiley & Sons Canada, Ltd, 22 Worcester Road, Rexdale, Ontario M9W 1L1.

In the United Kingdom and Europe, write to: Textbook Manager, John Wiley & Sons, Ltd., Baffins Lane, Chichester, Sussex PO 19 1UD, England.

Chapter 1

Introduction to Micro Focus Personal COBOL™

COBOL: A Valuable Language to Know

Micro Focus Personal COBOL: A Wise Investment

Personal COBOL: A Full-Featured Productivity Tool

COBOL: A Valuable Language to Know

COBOL is considered by many people to be the most successful computer programming language of all time. It has been used on a global scale for over 30 years by thousands of programmers to develop millions of business applications worth trillions of dollars.

The word COBOL is an acronym for *COmmon Business Oriented Language*. It is considered to be common in the sense that it may be used with almost every computer. Also, because it has been standardized, COBOL is used the same way regardless of the computer being programmed. As a result, programs developed in COBOL are easily transported from one computer to another. COBOL is considered to be business oriented because it is specifically designed to easily store, retrieve, manipulate, and report data in the manner typically needed by business information systems. COBOL is a real language, not only in the sense that it is used to communicate with a computer, but also because it has an English-like syntax, unlike others that are based on symbols and numbers.

COBOL was first developed in the late 1950s. One of the reasons COBOL has survived over so many years is that it has continued to evolve. The American National Standards Institute (ANSI) has an ongoing committee whose members represent computer manufacturers, compiler developers, and COBOL users. This committee is responsible for developing and publishing revisions to the COBOL standard. The current standard, ANS X3.23-1985, is most often referred to as COBOL 85. New features have been added periodically to enable COBOL to remain useful, even though computing technology and processing requirements have changed. This continues to be true today. Work is nearing completion on the next version of the COBOL standard. There have already been some additional language features approved for inclusion in the next version. Object-oriented programming (OOP) is a set of new programming techniques that many people feel will be widely used in the near future. Features necessary to permit COBOL to be used for object-oriented programming have been proposed for inclusion in the next standard version.

Well-designed programs developed in COBOL are much easier to modify and enhance than are programs developed in many other languages. This is important because the dynamic nature of the business world tends to result in continually changing information requirements. As needs have changed over the years, business information systems have had to keep pace by having their COBOL programs changed. It is common for applications developers to spend 70 to 80 percent of their time making modifications and enhancements to existing programs.

All of these factors make it likely that there will continue to be a large demand for business information systems development personnel who know COBOL. As a result, COBOL programmers should continue to experience the high salaries, job security, and career opportunities that have been prevalent for so many years.

Micro Focus Personal COBOL: A Wise Investment

Micro Focus is the world leader in providing COBOL development tools. Micro Focus has been the major supplier of COBOL compilers for many years. The company has been a very active participant in the standardization efforts associated with COBOL. Micro Focus is currently playing a leadership role in the development of the object-oriented version of COBOL. In recent years, the company has also been marketing software development tools designed to make computer programmers more productive. Micro Focus was the first to make available a program testing and debugging tool that displays COBOL source code during program execution.

Micro Focus Personal COBOL has been specifically designed to improve the productivity of those who are learning COBOL or who wish to develop personal applications. Many teachers of COBOL programming report that their students can develop their programs more quickly and with fewer errors as a result of using Personal COBOL.

Personal COBOL: A Full-Featured Productivity Tool

Personal COBOL has everything needed to develop COBOL programs as well as to execute them once they are completed. The following is a brief description of the major components of Personal COBOL.

SOFTWARE COMPONENTS

- **EDITOR**

When Personal COBOL is started, the Editor is the first component to appear. The Editor is used primarily for entering and modifying the various parts of a COBOL program. It has many features that make this easy to do. The Editor may also be used to create files containing program test data.

- **CHECKER**

The Checker component is used to compile a COBOL program. The compiler converts COBOL program statements into those to be used by the computer when the program is executed. The COBOL compiler included with Checker completely supports the ANSI 85 COBOL standard at the High Level (as defined by the U.S. Federal Government Standard). It also supports some very useful Micro Focus extensions to this standard.

- **ANIMATOR**

Animator is an interactive COBOL program testing and debugging tool. It is used to control the execution of a COBOL program that has been compiled by Checker to see if it will process correctly. It permits the programmer to monitor the execution of COBOL instructions as computer processing is accomplished. It also permits the programmer to see how the values of selected data items change as processing proceeds. These interactive capabilities are extremely useful for identifying which COBOL instructions need to be changed if the program does not behave as intended.

- **HYHELP**

HYHELP is the name given to the On-line Help System component of Personal COBOL. It may be used in two ways. One is to display information on the screen about how to use the major components of Personal COBOL such as Editor, Checker, or Animator. It may also be used to display technical information about the COBOL language, error messages, and other aspects of programming.

- **PCOBRUN**

Pcobrun may be used to execute a COBOL program after its development is complete. After a program has been compiled by Checker and found to be working properly, Pcobrun may be used to execute it from the operating system prompt. It is easier and faster to run a finished program in this way than it is to use the Animator within Personal COBOL.

SUPPORT COMPONENTS

- ***PROGRAMMER'S GUIDE***

Included with Personal COBOL is a *Programmer's Guide*. It contains over 325 pages of detailed information about Personal COBOL and how to use it. It contains some of the same information that may be found using HYHELP. However, the *Programmer's Guide* contains more detailed information on some topics and is organized differently. Some people find that they can get their questions answered more quickly using the guide, while others prefer to use the on-line help feature.

- **SAMPLE PROGRAMS**

Included with the files on the disks that are supplied with the Personal COBOL package are several sample programs. These programs demonstrate various advanced features of the Personal COBOL System as well as how some COBOL language features and Library Routines might be used. These sample programs are probably most useful to someone who is already familiar with the COBOL language.

- **TECHNICAL SUPPORT**

For those who have a modem as part of their personal computer configuration, there is technical support available through CompuServe and the Personal COBOL Special Interest Group (SIG) bulletin board operated by Micro Focus. These support services may be used to send and receive mail with other Personal COBOL users, report problems experienced with Personal COBOL, and express suggestions or concerns related to using Personal COBOL. Micro Focus encourages the submission of any ideas on how this product might be improved. The file named **`README.DOC`** on Disk 1 of the system package contains detailed information on how to use these support facilities. This file may be printed using an operating system command. If Disk 1 has been placed in Drive A, entering either **`TYPE A:README.DOC >PRN`** or **`PRINT A:README.DOC`** at the DOS prompt should result in this file being printed. It is about ten pages in length and contains other valuable information in addition to that related to using the support facilities.

The Micro Focus Personal COBOL System contains many useful features. Novice programmers as well as experienced professionals have found these features to be comprehensive, easy to learn, and easy to use.

Chapter 2

Installing Micro Focus Personal COBOL

Getting Ready

Installing Micro Focus Personal COBOL is simple and straightforward. Personal COBOL includes a program called Setup that provides step-by-step instructions on how to accomplish this process. However, there are a few things that should be done before beginning the installation.

• Confirm Availability of Minimum Computing Resources

Personal COBOL requires that certain hardware and software be available before it may be installed and used. The hardware required is an IBM personal computer or compatible with an 80286 CPU or higher and at least 640 kilobytes of RAM. At least 500 kilobytes of RAM must be available after the operating system and any resident utilities have been loaded. Also required is at least three megabytes of available hard disk space and at least one floppy disk drive. The software needed is DOS version 3.3 or higher. Personal COBOL may be run as a character-based, full-screen DOS application under Windows 3.0 or higher. The CHKDSK operating system command may be used to find out if there is enough hard disk space and free RAM. To

```
C:\>chkdsk
Volume Serial Number is 1889-283B

 159780864 bytes total disk space
     77824 bytes in 2 hidden files
    458752 bytes in 102 directories
  99381248 bytes in 4254 user files
     36864 bytes in bad sectors
  59826176 bytes available on disk      ◄ Available Disk Space

      4096 bytes in each allocation unit
     39009 total allocation units on disk
     14606 available allocation units on disk

    655360 total bytes memory
    625072 bytes free             ◄ Available RAM

C:\>
```

Figure 2.1 *Typical screen display produced by the DOS CHKDSK command.*

accomplish this, begin by turning on the computer or, if it is already on, rebooting the system by pressing either the reset button or pressing CTRL + ALT + DEL. Assuming Personal COBOL is to be installed on Drive C, enter **CHKDSK C:** at the DOS prompt. A status report similar to the one shown in Figure 2.1 will then be displayed. It identifies how many bytes are available on Drive C. At the bottom of the report are two lines that identify how many bytes of total memory (RAM) have been installed and how many of those bytes are free.

• Check the Personal COBOL Package Contents

The Personal COBOL System package should contain one book and two 3.5" high density floppy disks. The book is the *Programmer's Guide for Personal COBOL 2.0 for DOS.* The disks contain the files that make up the Personal COBOL System. On the disk labeled **Disk 1—SETUP and System 1** there is a file named **PCOBPAK.LST**. This file contains information about the disks and files contained in the package. It is recommended that this file be printed and read to check that the correct disks have been included in the package. A simple way to do this is to place Disk 1 into a drive and use the operating system TYPE or PRINT command. If Disk 1 was placed in Drive A, the file may be printed by entering either **TYPE A:PCOBPAK.LST >PRN** or **PRINT A:PCOBPAK.LST** at the DOS prompt.

- **Make Backup Copies of the Personal COBOL Disks**

It is always a good idea to protect software by making backup copies. It is recommended that the original disks be copied and then the copies be used during the installation process. This way if something goes wrong during the installation process that damages the files on the disks, the originals are still intact. Each disk may be copied using the DISKCOPY operating system command. For example, if the disk to be copied is placed in Drive A, entering **DISKCOPY A: A:** at the DOS prompt will initiate the copying process. The instructions necessary for swapping disks in the drive will be displayed on the screen at appropriate times during the copying process. As each disk is copied it should be labeled to indicate which of the Personal COBOL disks it is.

Installation Options

There are very few options available during the installation process. Each of these options has a default value. A default value is one that is used unless a different value is entered. The default values chosen for Personal COBOL are typically the ones most people would select. It is recommended that they be used when appropriate to avoid problems as well as to simplify the installation process.

Some people may be installing Personal COBOL on a system that already contains other Micro Focus software products. There are also those who have sophisticated systems and significant experience in installing software who may wish to control the details of how Personal COBOL is installed. In addition, there may be systems with marginal amounts of hard disk space available that require an installation restricted to only the minimum necessary components of Personal COBOL. For anyone facing any of these circumstances, it is recommended that they review Chapter 2 in the *Programmer's Guide* prior to beginning the installation process. In addition, there is a document file on Disk 1 of the system that should be printed and read. This file is named **README.DOC** and contains information called Release Notes, which supplement Chapter 2 of the *Programmer's Guide*. This information is particularly valuable for people who wish to customize their installation or for people whose printers are not attached to the LPT1 port. The **README.DOC** file may be printed using the same procedure as described in the previous section for printing the **PCOBPAK.LST** file.

Installing Personal COBOL

Assuming the default choices are satisfactory, the installation process may be accomplished in only a few minutes by performing the steps outlined below. If a customized installation is required, follow the steps given in Chapter 2 of the *Programmer's Guide* and the Release Notes in the **README.DOC** file. The installation process may be terminated at any time by pressing the [ESC] key.

1. Place the copy of the disk labeled **Disk 1—SETUP and System 1** into a floppy disk drive. Make this drive current by entering its letter followed by a colon. For example, if you placed Disk 1 into Drive A, type **A:** then press the Enter (↵) key. (In this manual, "enter" and "by entering" mean to type in the specified characters and then press the ↵ key.)

2. Execute the Setup program by entering **SETUP**.

3. Read the introductory screen and press the ↵ key to continue.

4. The screen should contain a display like the one in Figure 2.2. Carefully enter the name in which the Personal COBOL license is to be registered (usually your name) and check it as being correct. Only one opportunity is given to establish the name of registration. Once continuing past this step, it is not possible to change the name. Enter **Y** when the name is correct.

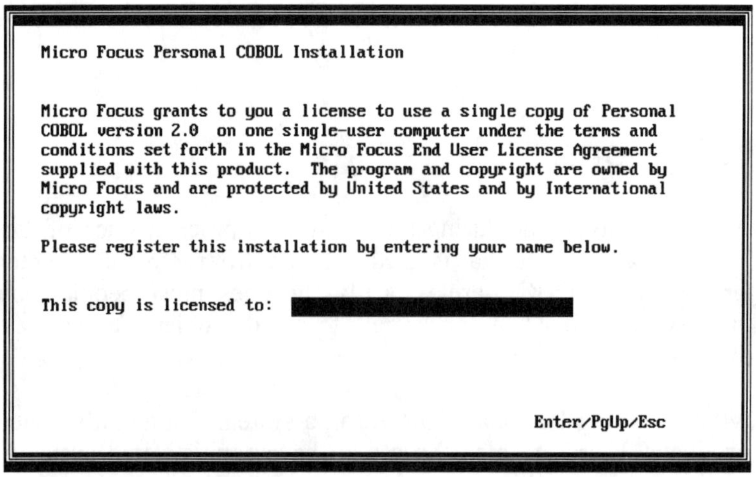

Figure 2.2 *Display used to request entry of the name in which the Personal COBOL license is to be registered.*

5. Next, an opportunity is provided to read the Release Notes given in the **README.DOC** file. You may skip this by pressing the [↓] key once and then pressing the ↵ key to continue.

6. Setup then asks which of the system's files are to be installed. Accept the default to install all of them by pressing the ↵ key.

7. The hard disk directories to be used for storing the system's files are established next. Accept each of the defaults (**C:\MFCOBOL** and **C:\MFCOBOL\SAMPLES**) by pressing the ↵ key and verifying by pressing the **Y** key.

8. Setup then checks to see if there is sufficient disk space on the specified hard disk to install the system's files. If there is, installation continues. If not, an opportunity is given to change the specified drive.

9. Setup continues by copying the system's files from the floppy disks to the hard disk. The names of the files are displayed on the screen as they are copied. Many of the files have been stored on the floppy disks using a compressed or "zipped" format so that each disk can hold a greater number of files. This results in fewer disks being required to hold all of the files in the Personal COBOL System. When one of these zipped files is copied to the hard disk, the display indicates that it is being "unzipped." When all of the files on Disk 1 have been copied, Setup asks for Disk 2 to be placed into the floppy drive, and copies its files. After Disk 2 has had its files copied, Setup asks that Disk 1 again be placed in the floppy drive. Simply follow the instructions on the screen to swap disks when requested.

10. The final task that the Setup program needs to accomplish is to make necessary entries into the **AUTOEXEC.BAT** and **CONFIG.SYS** operating system files. These files are used during the computer startup processing to perform initialization tasks that tailor the operating environment of the computer. When Setup asks for permission to do this, enter **Y**.

11. Setup ends with an instruction that the system needs to be rebooted by pressing [CTRL] + [ALT] + [DEL]. This is so that the changes made to the **AUTOEXEC.BAT** and **CONFIG.SYS** files will take effect. *Remove Disk 1 from the floppy drive and then reboot. Personal COBOL should now be installed and ready for use.*

Verifying the Installation

Once the system has been rebooted at the end of the installation process, it is wise to quickly check that it is working correctly. This may be done simply by entering **PCOBOL** at the DOS prompt. If the system is working correctly, the Personal COBOL Banner should be displayed on the screen. Except for the name to whom the system is licensed, the banner should appear similar to the one in Figure 2.3. If it does, press any key and the Editor Windowand Main Menu should appear. They should appear similar to the ones in Figure 2.4. If either of these screens do not appear as they should, then something has gone wrong with the installation process or minimum

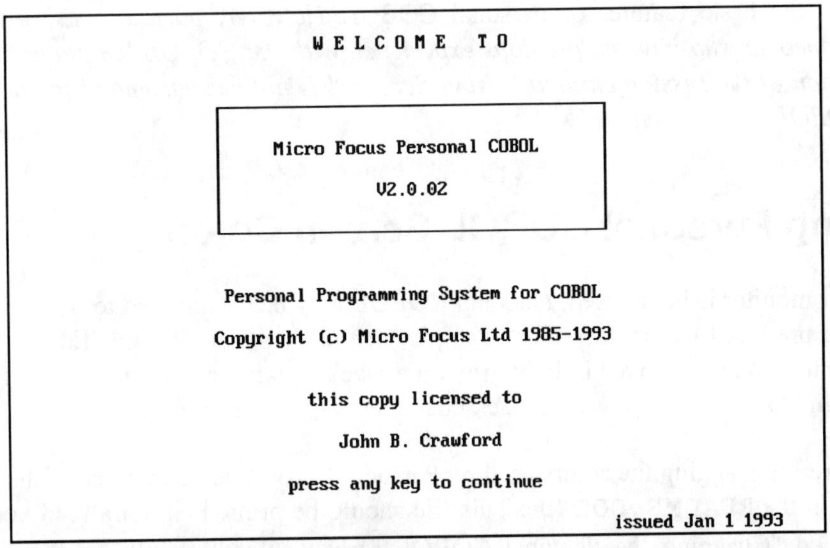

Figure 2.3 *Typical banner display appearing each time Personal COBOL is activated.*

computing resources are not available. In this case, review Chapter 2 of the *Programmer's Guide* and the Release Notes in the **README.DOC** file for ideas on how to correct the problem and reinstall the system.

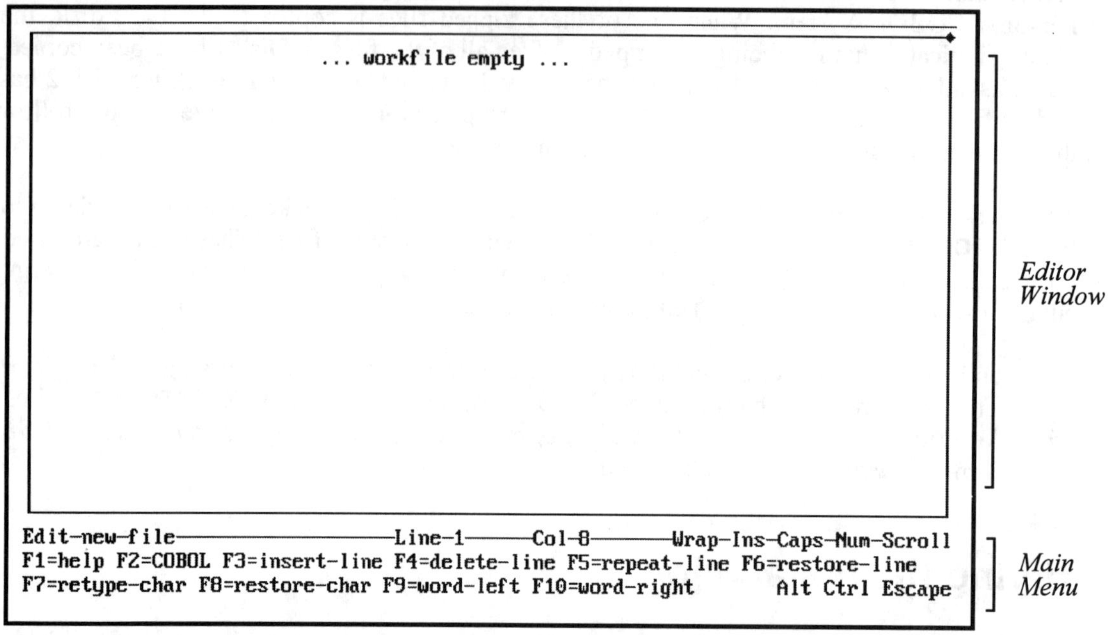

Figure 2.4 *Editor Window and Main Menu that should appear if installation was successful and minimum computing resources are available.*

If Personal COBOL is working correctly, two choices may be made at this point. One choice is to end execution of Personal COBOL and return to the operating system. This may be accomplished by pressing the ESC key. The other choice is to begin the Sample Session provided in Chapter 3 of the *Programmer's Guide*. The Sample Session is one way for COBOL users to become familiar with the basic features of Personal COBOL. *However, parts of this session may be confusing to people who have no previous experience with the COBOL language. In particular, the last portion of the session entitled "Using Screens" is not recommended for people with no previous COBOL background.*

Changing Personal COBOL Screen Colors

When a color monitor is being used, Personal COBOL may be customized to display some things in the colors preferred by its user. For example, in the Personal COBOL Editor Window, the default is for text to be displayed in light grey on a black background. Some people may prefer to reverse this and have text displayed as black characters on a light gray background.

The procedure for changing the colors used by Personal COBOL are explained within the Release Notes given in the **README.DOC** file. This file should be printed (if not already done) and the section entitled "Changing the Personal COBOL screen colors" should be reviewed prior to attempting any color changes.

The color specifications for Personal COBOL are contained in the file named **PCOBOL.CFG**. This file may be edited (changed) using any text editing software, including the Personal COBOL Editor. The screen color specifications are located in the section entitled "[PCOBOL-ATTRIBUTES]" of **PCOBOL.CFG**. The screen attributes are listed along with their current values and primary purpose.

The customizing procedure is simply to modify the current attribute values to the ones desired. For example, changing the attribute identified as SYS-ATT-11 from "LIGHT-GREY ON BLACK" to "BLACK ON LIGHT-GREY" will result in reversing the colors used to display text in the Editor Window.

The backup procedures described in the Release Notes should be followed prior to making any changes. It is recommended that extensive color changes not be made until some experience has been gained in using Personal COBOL. Care needs to be taken not to modify other portions of the **PCOBOL.CFG** *file or Personal COBOL may not work correctly.*

Chapter 3

The Program Development Process

Computer Programming

A primary component of every business information system is the set of computer programs making up its software. A computer program is a set of instructions to be carried out by a computer. The process of developing computer programs is called computer programming and the people who perform this process are called computer programmers. Part of this development process involves using a computer programming language to specify the necessary instructions.

There are two major types of computer programming languages used to develop business information systems: procedural and nonprocedural. A procedural programming language is sometimes referred to as a third generation language while a nonprocedural language is often referred to as fourth generation language (4GL). The primary difference between these two types of languages is found in the level of detail that the computer programmer must provide. Nonprocedural languages are less detailed because they are used to specify *what* processing is required. Procedural languages are more detailed because they must specify *how* to perform required processing. Nonprocedural languages are considered to be higher-level languages because it generally does not take as much detail to specify *what* to do as it does to specify *how* to do it. For example, it is much easier to tell someone to unload a truck than it is to tell them how to do all the steps involved in the unloading process. On the surface, therefore, it would seem that nonprocedural languages are better because they require less detail and take less time to write. But sometimes it is important to be able to control exactly how processing is done. In these cases, procedural languages provide that capability where nonprocedural languages do not.

COBOL is a procedural programming language. It is the most widely used language for business information systems development. Other procedural languages include BASIC, PASCAL, Ada, C, PL/1, and FORTRAN. One of the most widely used nonprocedural languages is Structured Query Language or SQL (sometimes pronounced *sequel*). SQL is currently the only 4GL that has an ANSI standard. Other nonprocedural languages include FOCUS, NOMAD, and RAMIS. Many people consider database languages like dBASE IV and ACCESS to also be nonprocedural.

The program development process is basically the same regardless of the type of language being used. The primary steps involved are understanding processing requirements, constructing the program, and testing the program. However, procedural programming generally includes some extra planning because of the greater detail required. The remainder of this chapter will be devoted to explaining the program development process in more detail and identifying the components of Micro Focus Personal COBOL that may be used in this process.

Understanding Program Requirements

Understanding what a computer program is supposed to do is the most important step in the program development process. Without a clear understanding of program requirements, it is impossible to develop a useful program. There are three basic areas that must be understood to develop a computer program: the output that must be produced, the input available, and the procedures necessary to convert the input into the output. In many organizations, these are specified as part of the design phase of the systems development process by someone with a title such as Systems Analyst, Systems Designer, Programmer Analyst, or Systems Engineer.

Most programmers find that the easiest way to begin understanding requirements is to become familiar with the output expected from the program. This output might be a printed report, a screen display, a file, or some combination of these. Each report or display should be specified in a way that identifies the content, placement, and editing of its titles, subtitles, side headings, column headings, captions, footings, data items, and calculation results. Each file needs to be specified in a way that identifies its label, access method, and record length, as well as the order, field size, and data type of its data items. Understanding the output provides a clear focus on what the program is supposed to do.

Understanding the input is probably the next most useful area with which to become familiar. The majority of a program's input comes from either data records retrieved from files or keyboard entries made by the user of the program. Input files should be specified in the same way output files are specified. Each keyboard entry is usually specified by describing its data types and field size along with a description of the possible values that might be entered. Understanding the input to a program provides a clear idea of what is available for use in creating the required output.

The final area to understand is the procedures required to convert the input into output. A lot of this may be obvious and not require much, if any, description. Names, dates, times, identifying numbers, and prices are examples of business data items that require little or no processing to convert them from their input form to their output form. However, some procedures are not obvious and must be described. Procedures like this might include how calculation results are derived, how data is summarized, which data is selected for processing, and how to check for data errors. Understanding these procedures completes the process of becoming familiar with program requirements.

Planning Program Logic

The instructions used to compose a computer program must be organized in a manner to insure that the computer does the right thing at the right time. They must also be organized in a way that makes the program easy to understand and modify. This organization pattern is referred to as the program's logic. The program logic determines which processing tasks will be accomplished and how the execution of those tasks will be controlled. One of the biggest challenges in computer programming is determining how to control the execution of program instructions. When a procedural programming language like COBOL is used to develop a computer program, the program logic must be planned.

A well-structured program is made up of logical modules. Each logical module consists of a group of instructions designed to carry out a specific processing task. There are two basic types of logical modules, worker modules and manager modules. A worker module is made up primarily of instructions used to process data. Examples of worker modules might include those used to get a record from an input file, perform a specific calculation, or print a title on a report. A manager module consists primarily of instructions used to control the execution of other manager or worker modules. These two types of logical modules serve as building blocks for constructing a program's logic.

The execution of logical modules is controlled by program features called logical control structures. There are three basic ways to control the execution of logical modules: sequence, iteration, and selection. (There is a special form of the selection control structure called the case structure that is considered by some to be a fourth logical control structure.) The sequence control structure is the simplest. It means to execute the logical modules in the order they are specified. The iteration control structure is used when a logical module needs to be executed over and over again until some condition is satisfied. Sometimes a program must perform one type of processing under some conditions and another type under different conditions. The selection control structure is used when a decision must be made regarding which logical modules to select for execution.

One highly recommended tool that may be used to plan program logic is called a hierarchy chart. The hierarchy chart is based on the concept of the organization chart used in business to show the management hierarchy of a company or similar organization. Figure 3.1 illustrates a partially

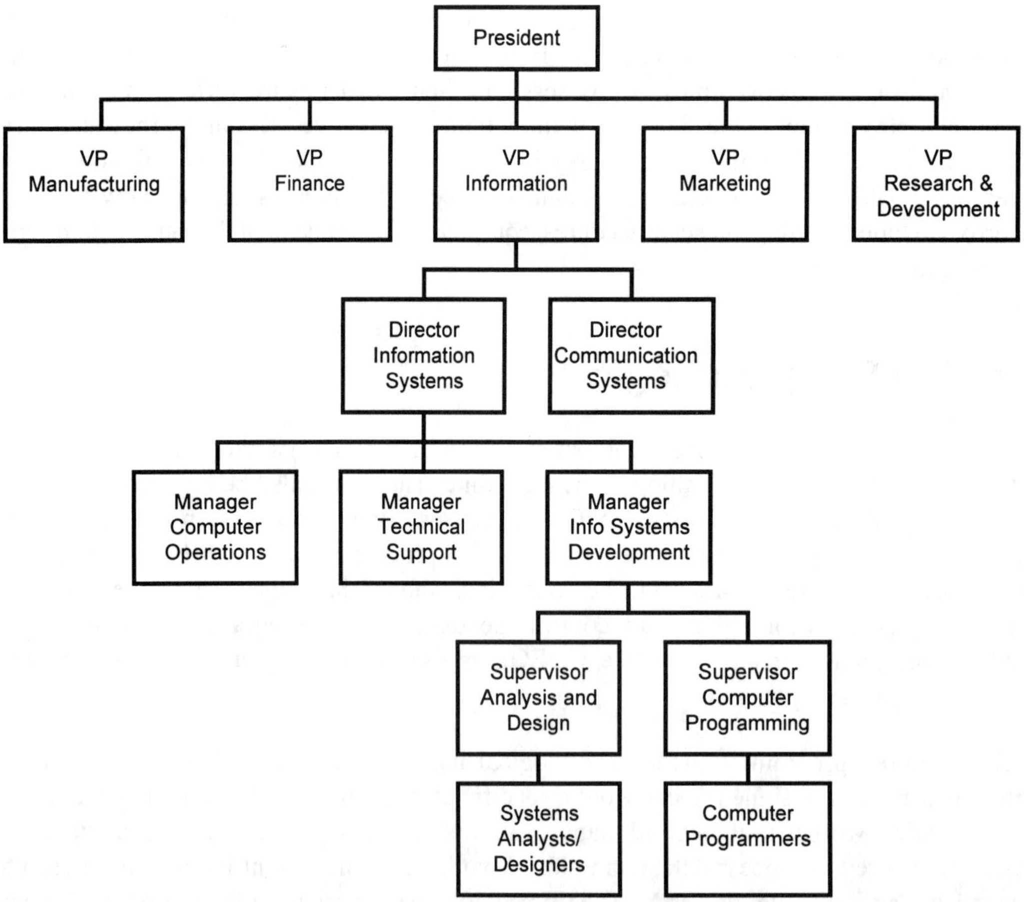

Figure 3.1 *Partially completed organization chart showing the hierarchy of management typically used to control business functions.*

completed organization chart. Most organizations have one person at the top who serves as the president or chief executive officer. On the next management level are the vice presidents whose activities are controlled by the president. The vice presidents control the activities of the directors, the directors control the managers, the managers control the supervisors, and so on. At the bottom of the hierarchy are the workers.

Because the logical modules of a program may be thought of as managers and workers, this same approach may be used to organize and control them. Figure 3.2 illustrates the typical features of a hierarchy chart. This chart depicts the logical modules that might be used to construct a program that accumulates and lists data from a file. Each box on the chart represents either a manager or worker module. The lines between the boxes indicate which modules are being controlled by which other modules. The slash in the upper-right corner of a box indicates that a module is the same as one appearing elsewhere on the chart.

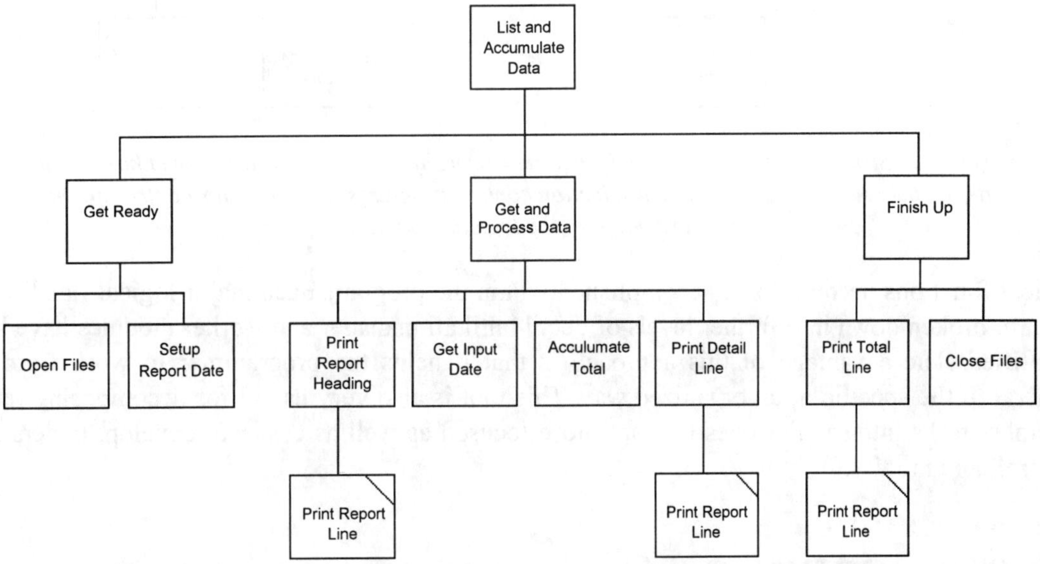

Figure 3.2 *Heirarchy chart of logical modules planned for a program that accumulates and lists data from a file.*

Although the hierarchy chart identifies the logical modules of a program and which ones are controlling others, it does not specify which logical constructs are being used to control the execution of the modules. Some people use an enhanced form of hierarch chart, called a structure chart, to identify the control structures used in a program's logic. Figure 3.3 illustrates how the hierarchy chart in Figure 3.2 may be enhanced to show the sequence, iteration, and selection control stuctures used. Sequence is indicated by placing the boxes in left-to-right order in the sequence they should be executed. Iteration is indicated by placing a curved arrow above a module that needs to be executed repeatedly. Selection is indicated by placing a small diamond above those modules that are executed only when certain conditions exist.

One of the advantages of using hierarchy or structure charts to design program logic is that it is done in a top-down fashion. The box at the top is placed first and represents the program's main logical function. The boxes on the next level are determined next and represent each of the major

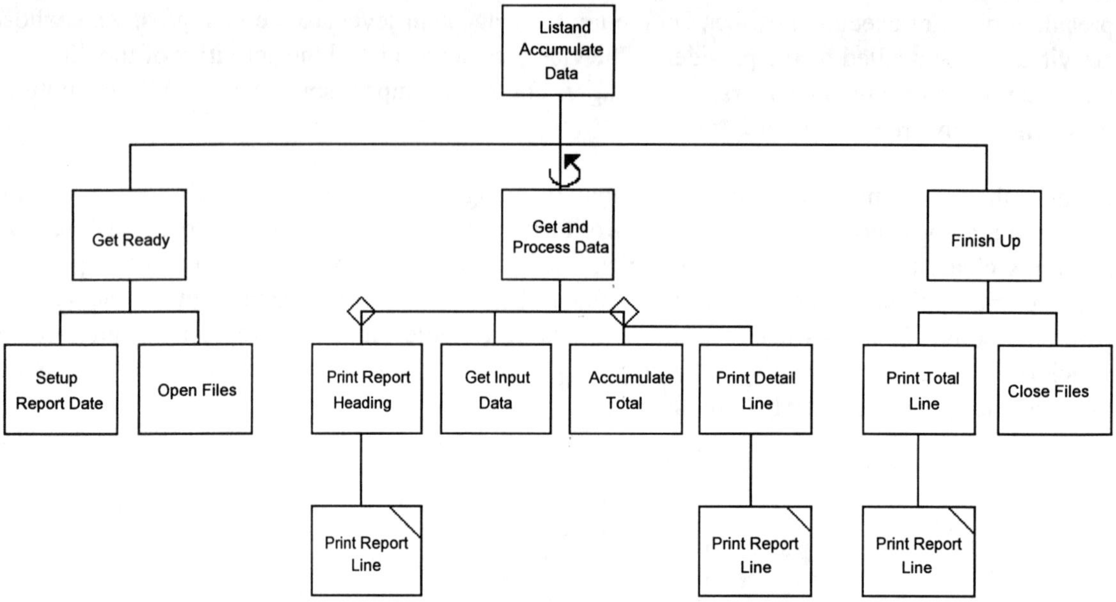

Figure 3.3 *Structure chart constructed from the heirarchy chart in Figure 3.2 by enhancing it to depict the sequence, iteration, and selection control structures to be used for controlling the execution of the logical modules.*

logical functions needing to be accomplished within the program. Each major logical function is, in turn, broken down into further levels of detail until all manager and worker modules have been identified. The advantage of this approach is that it helps the programmer to work from the general to the specific in an organized way. This tool is also very useful for decomposing rather complex tasks into smaller ones that are more focused as well as easier to develop, understand, control, and modify.

Writing a COBOL Program

A typical COBOL program has four main parts called divisions. The IDENTIFICATION DIVISION appears first in a COBOL program and may be used to identify the program and its author. Comments regarding program purpose or a log of program changes is also often included in this division. The ENVIRONMENT DIVISION is used primarily for identifying the input and output files the program will use. The DATA DIVISION is used to describe the data that will be processed by the program. It is usually composed of two sections. The FILE SECTION is where the fields and records of the input and/or output files are described. The WORKING-STORAGE SECTION is used to describe places in memory for storing control fields, calculation results, and constants, and for temporary holding areas. The PROCEDURE DIVISION is used to specify the instructions that tell the computer how to process the data described in the DATA DIVISION. The PROCEDURE DIVISION is composed of paragraphs. The paragraphs are the logical modules of the program. Each paragraph contains instructions to perform a specific manager or worker function and should correspond to one of the boxes on the structure chart used to plan the program's logic. Figure 3.4 contains a three-page listing of a COBOL program based on the structure chart shown in Figure 3.3.

Every programming language has certain rules that must be followed when writing a program. These rules are called language syntax rules and they control how the various features of the language must be specified. For example, COBOL requires that division, section, and paragraph names begin somewhere in the 8th through 11th positions of a line. Most other COBOL statements may begin in positions 12 through 72.

The process of writing a program is begun by creating a file containing all of the program statements necessary to specify what the program is required to do and how it is supposed to do it. The records in this file must be constructed in a particular way and contain statements that conform to the language syntax rules. This file, often referred to as a source code file, is created using a text editing program. This process is just like using a word processing program to create a document. However, most word processors and general purpose text editing programs are not set up to make it easy to enter the statements of any particular programming language.

The Micro Focus Personal COBOL System includes a module called Editor that is specifically designed to make it easy to enter COBOL statements, create new COBOL source code files, and modify existing COBOL source code files. Editor is the first feature to appear when Personal COBOL is activated. It recognizes COBOL source code files and automatically sets record characteristics, margins, tab settings, and other options to conform to COBOL requirements. It is also designed to facilitate the inserting, duplicating, modifying, deleting, and moving of COBOL statements. Another feature of Personal COBOL that facilitates writing COBOL programs is the Language Reference aid available through the On-line Help System. It displays diagrams on the screen that depict the required and optional portions of COBOL language statements.

An introduction to using the Personal COBOL Editor is contained in Chapter 4 of this manual. A full description of Editor's features is contained in Chapter 4 of the *Programmer's Guide.* The Language Reference feature is discussed in Chapter 9 of the *Programmer's Guide*.

Compiling COBOL Source Code

After a COBOL program has been created with Editor, it must be converted from the COBOL language to the language understood by the computer that will be executing the program (called the target or object computer). Each make of computer understands only one language. This language is usually referred to as machine language or object code. There are several different machine languages. Each computer manufacturer tends to have its own machine language that is different from that of other computer manufacturers. It is very difficult to write programs in machine languages. They tend to be composed of letters, numbers, and special symbols that resemble an encrypted code more than they do a language. Standardized languages like COBOL are much easier to use and, because they are standardized, are the same regardless of which computer is being programmed. But since computers understand machine language only and do not understand standard languages, the source code of a program must be translated into the object code of the target computer.

```
* Micro Focus Personal COBOL v2.0.02 L2.0 revision 002 23-Nov-93 03:59 Page 1
*                                                SAMPLE.CBL
* Options: WB EDITOR(MF) LIST() ANIM ENSUITE(2) CONFIRM
 IDENTIFICATION DIVISION.
   PROGRAM-ID.  SAMPLE.
   AUTHOR.      John B. Crawford.
*  PURPOSE.     List and accumulate data from an input file.
 ENVIRONMENT DIVISION.
 INPUT-OUTPUT SECTION.
 FILE-CONTROL.
     SELECT SAMPLE-DATA      ASSIGN "SAMPLE.DAT"
                             ORGANIZATION IS LINE SEQUENTIAL.
     SELECT SAMPLE-REPORT    ASSIGN "SAMPLE.RPT".
/
 DATA DIVISION.
 FILE SECTION.
 FD  SAMPLE-DATA.
 01  INPUT-RECORD.
     02  IN-NAME             PIC X(20).
     02  IN-AMOUNT           PIC 9(04).
 FD  SAMPLE-REPORT.
 01  PRINT-RECORD.
     02  LEFT-MARGIN         PIC X(20).
     02  PRINT-AREA          PIC X(40).
 WORKING-STORAGE SECTION.
 01  REPORT-LINES.
     02  TITLE-LINE          PIC X(40)
           VALUE "             SAMPLE REPORT               ".
     02  SUBTITLE-LINE.
         03  REPORT-DATE.
             04  RPT-MMDD    PIC XX/XX/.
             04  RPT-YY      PIC XX.
         03  FILLER          PIC X(25)   VALUE SPACES.
         03  FILLER          PIC X(05)   VALUE "PAGE ".
         03  RPT-PAGE-NO     PIC Z9.
     02  COLUMN-HEADING-LINE PIC X(40)
           VALUE "      Name                  Amount     ".
     02  DETAIL-LINE.
         03  FILLER          PIC X(05)   VALUE SPACES.
         03  RPT-NAME        PIC X(20).
         03  FILLER          PIC X(04)   VALUE SPACES.
         03  RPT-AMOUNT      PIC ZZ,ZZ9.
         03  FILLER          PIC X(05)   VALUE SPACES.
     02  TOTAL-LINE.
```

Figure 3.4a *Listing of COBOL source code based on structure chart in Figure 3.3, page 1 of 3.*

```
* Micro Focus Personal COBOL v2.0.02 L2.0 revision 002 23-Nov-93 03:59 Page 2
*                                        SAMPLE.CBL
               03  FILLER           PIC X(20)    VALUE SPACES.
               03  FILLER           PIC X(07)    VALUE "TOTAL  ".
               03  RPT-TOTAL        PIC $ZZZ,ZZ9.
               03  FILLER           PIC X(05)    VALUE SPACES.

       01  CONTROLS-AND-HOLDING-AREAS.
           02  END-OF-FILE          PIC X(05)    VALUE "FALSE".
           02  TODAYS-DATE-HOLD.
               03  TODAY-YY         PIC X(02).
               03  TODAY-MMDD       PIC X(04).
           02  REQD                 PIC 9(02).

       01  ACCUMULATORS.
           02  TOTAL-AMOUNT         PIC S9(6)    VALUE ZERO.
           02  LINE-COUNT           PIC S9(2)    VALUE +99.
           02  PAGE-COUNT           PIC S9(2)    VALUE ZERO.
      /
       PROCEDURE DIVISION.


       LIST-AND-ACCUM-DATA.
           PERFORM 1-GET-READY
           PERFORM 2-GET-AND-PROCESS-DATA
               UNTIL END-OF-FILE = "TRUE "
           PERFORM 3-FINISH-UP
           STOP RUN.



       1-GET-READY.
           PERFORM 11-SETUP-RPT-DATE-AND-MARGIN
           PERFORM 12-OPEN-FILES.

       11-SETUP-RPT-DATE-AND-MARGIN.
           ACCEPT TODAYS-DATE-HOLD      FROM DATE
           MOVE TODAY-MMDD              TO RPT-MMDD
           MOVE TODAY-YY                TO RPT-YY
           MOVE SPACES                  TO LEFT-MARGIN.

       12-OPEN-FILES.
           OPEN INPUT  SAMPLE-DATA
                OUTPUT SAMPLE-REPORT.



       2-GET-AND-PROCESS-DATA.
           IF LINE-COUNT > +53
               PERFORM 21-PRINT-REPORT-HEADING
               END-IF
           PERFORM 22-GET-INPUT-RECORD
           IF END-OF-FILE NOT = "TRUE "
               PERFORM 23-ACCUMULATE-TOTAL
               PERFORM 24-PRINT-DETAIL-LINE
               END-IF.

```

Figure 3.4b *Listing of COBOL source code based on structure chart in Figure 3.3, page 2 of 3.*

```
* Micro Focus Personal COBOL v2.0.02 L2.0 revision 002 23-Nov-93 03:59 Page 3
*                                     SAMPLE.CBL
 21-PRINT-REPORT-HEADING.
     MOVE TITLE-LINE               TO PRINT-AREA
     WRITE PRINT-RECORD AFTER ADVANCING PAGE
     MOVE +7                       TO LINE-COUNT
     ADD  +1                       TO PAGE-COUNT
     MOVE PAGE-COUNT               TO RPT-PAGE-NO
     MOVE SUBTITLE-LINE            TO PRINT-AREA
     MOVE 2                        TO REQD
     PERFORM 211-PRINT-REPORT-LINE
     MOVE COLUMN-HEADING-LINE      TO PRINT-AREA
     MOVE 3                        TO REQD
     PERFORM 211-PRINT-REPORT-LINE.

 211-PRINT-REPORT-LINE.
     WRITE PRINT-RECORD AFTER ADVANCING REQD LINES
     ADD REQD                      TO LINE-COUNT.
/
 22-GET-INPUT-RECORD.
     READ SAMPLE-DATA
       AT END
         MOVE "TRUE "              TO END-OF-FILE.

 23-ACCUMULATE-TOTAL.
     ADD IN-AMOUNT                 TO TOTAL-AMOUNT.

 24-PRINT-DETAIL-LINE.
     MOVE IN-NAME                  TO RPT-NAME
     MOVE IN-AMOUNT                TO RPT-AMOUNT
     MOVE DETAIL-LINE              TO PRINT-AREA
     PERFORM 211-PRINT-REPORT-LINE
     MOVE 2                        TO REQD.



 3-FINISH-UP.
     PERFORM 31-PRINT-TOTAL-LINE
     PERFORM 32-CLOSE-FILES.

 31-PRINT-TOTAL-LINE.
     MOVE TOTAL-AMOUNT             TO RPT-TOTAL
     MOVE TOTAL-LINE               TO PRINT-AREA
     MOVE 3                        TO REQD
     PERFORM 211-PRINT-REPORT-LINE.

 32-CLOSE-FILES.
     CLOSE SAMPLE-DATA
           SAMPLE-REPORT.


***** END OF SAMPLE PROGRAM SOURCE CODE *****


* Micro Focus Personal COBOL v2.0.02 L2.0 revision 002
*
* Total Messages:     0
* Data:        1232     Code:         547     Dictionary:        2167
```

Figure 3.4c *Listing of COBOL source code based on structure chart in Figure 3.3, page 3 of 3.*

When a program has been written in COBOL, a special program called a compiler must be used to translate the COBOL source code into the target computer's object code. The compiler reads the records in the source code file and examines the COBOL statements to see if they contain any syntax errors. The compiler produces an output report file called a source listing. This report lists all of the COBOL statements along with any syntax errors that are found. If no syntax errorsare found, the compiler produces an object code file containing machine language instructions equivalent to those specified in the COBOL program. The object code file is then used to execute the program on the target computer. If syntax errors are found, then the appropriate source code statements must be changed using an editor to remove the errors before another attempt to compile is made.

The Micro Focus Personal COBOL System includes a COBOL compiler called Checker. Once a COBOL source code file has been created and saved using Editor, Checker may be activated to perform syntax checking and object code compilation. Checker includes features that allow the source listing to be omitted, directed to a file, displayed on the screen, or printed. Checker may also be directed either to pause each time it finds a syntax error or to check the entire program without pausing. An option is also available directing Checker to produce a cross-reference listing that can be a useful aid for locating specific items in COBOL source code. When Checker discovers one or more syntax errors, it automatically reactivates Editor at the source code statement associated with the first error. A brief description of how to use Checker's basic features is in Chapter 5 of this manual. A more complete discussion of Checker is contained in Chapter 5 of the *Programmer's Guide*.

Developing Test Data

Once a COBOL program has been successfully compiled, it must be tested to see if it works properly. Many programs in business information systems are used to process data stored in files. Therefore, before a program can be tested, sample input files must be created that contain data representative of the type to be processed once the program is finished and placed into production.

Sample data files used in program testing are usually created with an editor in much the same way COBOL source code files are created. The Personal COBOL Editor may be used for this process. How this may be accomplished is discussed in Chapter 6 of this manual. Figure 3.5 is a list of sample data records in a test file that could be used to test the sample program shown in Figure 3.4. The first 20 positions of each record contain a company name and the next 4 positions contain a number representing a dollar amount.

Program Testing

A COBOL program may be tested after an object code file has been produced by the compiler and any required test data files have been created. This testing process is crucial to the program development process. There is nothing worse for a programmer's reputation as a professional than to place a program into production that does not work properly. To avoid this, every program must be very thoroughly tested. Recall that the compiler only checks to make sure that the source code statements have been written in a way that do not violate the language syntax rules. The compiler has no way of knowing which commands should be included in a program. So a source code file may contain correctly written statements, but not the ones that are appropriate for what the program is supposed to do. Errors in processing that result from a program having inappropriate statements are called logic errors. The process of testing and changing a program until it has no logic errors is often referred to as program debugging or logic debugging.

```
ADVANCED TECHNOLOGY 3616
BRAVADO SUPPLIERS   1947
COMPLETE EVERYTHING 0175
DELPHI FACTORIES    2011
ECHOTECH, LTD.      8737
FASTER FOREVER      0139
GROOVEY, INC.       4542
HASTEN 2 U          2689
INNOVATIVE PARTS    6405
JAGS R US           3651
JUMBO INDUSTRIAL    7524
KILOCOMP CORP.      7320
KWIKTECH, INC.      5432
LIMBO COMPONENTS    9734
MACHO MECHANO       6789
NIMBLE AGENTS       9527
OPTIMUM UNLIMITED   2645
PRECISION MFG.      0579
QUICKY IMPORTS      1083
RECLAIMED STUFF     3582
RELIABLE SUPPLY     5177
SECURITY PROVIDERS  2435
SUITABLE SUPPLIER   1827
TECHNIQUE BOUTIQUE  3687
ULTIMATE FACTORS    2482
VERIFIABLE SUPPLY   1623
WASTENOT LIMITED    0040
XEROMATIC CORP.     4914
YOUNGCO, INC.       3253
ZZYZZX TECHNOLOGIES 4524
```

Company Name *$ Amt*

Figure 3.5 *List of records in data file to be used to test the COBOL program in Figure 3.4. Each record contains a company name in positions 1–20 and a dollar amount in positions 21–24.*

By being familiar with the processing requirements and having a thorough understanding of the sample input data files, a programmer can determine the exact results that should be produced by the program being tested. For example, the test data shown in Figure 3.5 indicates that the program should list 30 lines with names and amounts. By using a calculator to add up the numbers it can be determined that the total at the end of the report should be 118,089. Once these results are determined, program debugging is accomplished by executing the program and comparing the results it produces with what it should have produced. If the results do not match, the program is modified and tested repeatedly until the correct results are produced. Figure 3.6 contains the two-page report produced by the sample program processing the sample data.

SAMPLE REPORT

11/23/93 PAGE 1

Name	Amount
ADVANCED TECHNOLOGY	3,616
BRAVADO SUPPLIERS	1,947
COMPLETE EVERYTHING	175
DELPHI FACTORIES	2,011
ECHOTECH, LTD.	8,737
FASTER FOREVER	139
GROOVEY, INC.	4,542
HASTEN 2 U	2,689
INNOVATIVE PARTS	6,405
JAGS R US	3,651
JUMBO INDUSTRIAL	7,524
KILOCOMP CORP.	7,320
KWIKTECH, INC.	5,432
LIMBO COMPONENTS	9,734
MACHO MECHANO	6,789
NIMBLE AGENTS	9,527
OPTIMUM UNLIMITED	2,645
PRECISION MFG.	579
QUICKY IMPORTS	1,083

SAMPLE REPORT

11/23/93 PAGE 2

Name	Amount
RECLAIMED STUFF	3,582
RELIABLE SUPPLY	5,177
SECURITY PROVIDERS	2,435
SUITABLE SUPPLIER	1,827
TECHNIQUE BOUTIQUE	3,687
ULTIMATE FACTORS	2,482
VERIFIABLE SUPPLY	1,623
WASTENOT LIMITED	40
XEROMATIC CORP.	4,914
YOUNGCO, INC.	3,253
ZZYZZX TECHNOLOGIES	4,524
TOTAL	$118,089

Figure 3.6 *Two-page report produced by the COBOL program in Figure 3.4 when it processed the data file listed in Figure 3.5.*

The Micro Focus Personal COBOL System includes a component called Animator that is a very helpful tool for program testing. It permits the programmer to view the source code statements as they are executed and to monitor processing results on a continuous and step-by-step basis. Often it is the case that a programmer knows a program is not doing the right thing, but has trouble locating the area of the program that is not correct. Animator provides the ability to follow a program's progress so that it is easier to spot which instructions in the program are producing the erroneous results. Using Animator for program testing is briefly discussed in Chapter 7 of this manual. A full discussion of Animator is available in Chapter 6 of the *Programmer's Guide*. The Micro Focus Personal COBOL System is designed to provide easy transitions between Editor, Checker, and Animator to facilitate the program testing process.

Summary of the Program Development Process

- Understand processing requirements by becoming familiar with program outputs, inputs, and procedures.
- Use a program structure chart to identify the logical modules needed and how they should be controlled.
- Create a COBOL source code file by entering the proper statements using the features of Editor and Language Reference.
- Compile the program using Checker and use Editor to correct any syntax errors.
- Use Editor to create any sample input data files required for testing.
- Determine what results to expect when the test data is processed.
- Use Animator to execute the program and monitor processing results. Compare output results with those expected. Use the Editor, Checker, and Animator repeatedly as required to modify and test the program until all logic errors are eliminated.

Chapter 4

Using the Personal COBOL Editor

Invoking the Personal COBOL Editor

The Personal COBOL Editor is the primary tool used to enter and modify the COBOL statements making up a source code file. This chapter will briefly explain the major features of Editor, concentrating on those most often used to develop COBOL programs. A complete description of all Editor features is located in Chapter 4 of the *Programmer's Guide*.

Once the Personal COBOL installation process has been completed successfully, invoking the Editor is very simple. The process usually begins by making the directory containing the Personal COBOL System the default directory. Next, the Personal COBOL System is executed in one of two ways. If a new source code file is to be created, entering **PCOBOL** at the DOS prompt will invoke Editor with an empty workspace. If an existing source code file is to be worked on, enter **PCOBOL** followed by a space and then the filename (for example, **PCOBOL SAMPLE.CBL**) to invoke Editor with the file loaded into the workspace. The first display screen to appear should be the copyright screen, which is acknowledged by pressing any key. The next screen to appear is the Editor screen.

The Editor Screen

The Editor screen is the primary display in the Personal COBOL system. It provides the space needed to enter and modify a COBOL program. It also provides access to the other features of the system. The Editor screen is composed of two major areas: the Work Areaand the Control Area. Figure 4.1 illustrates a typical Editor screen display

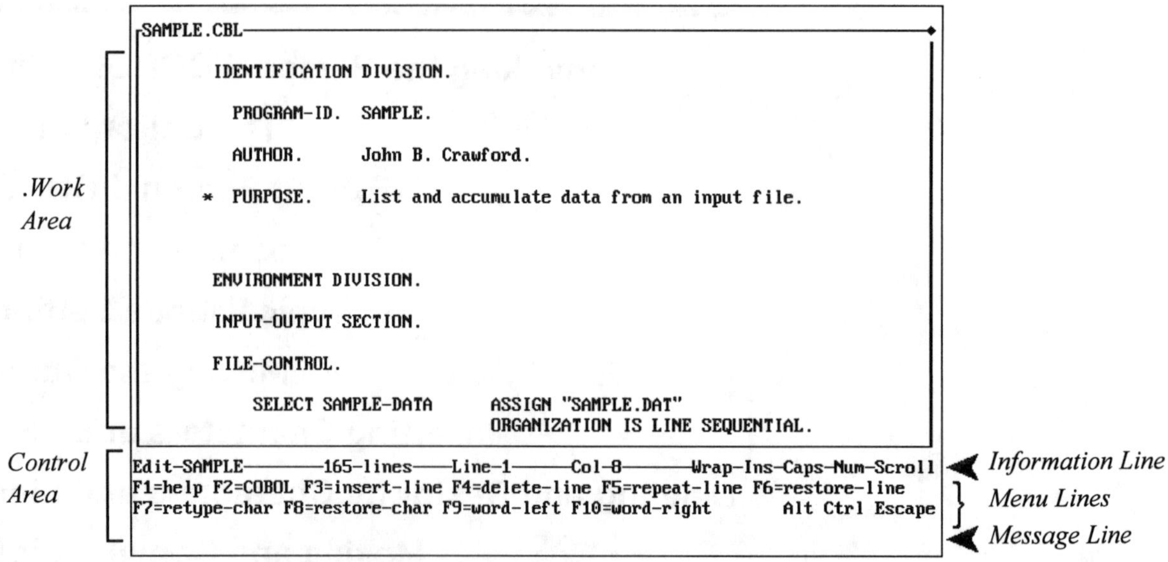

Figure 4.1 *Primary display of Editor showing Work Area loaded with a COBOL program and the Control Area with the Main Menu displayed.*

The Work Area is the window provided for entering and modifying COBOL statements. This area is used most in developing COBOL programs. If Personal COBOL is invoked to create a new COBOL program, this area will be empty except for the phrase **"...workfile empty..."**, which appears near the top of the screen. If Personal COBOL is invoked to work on an existing COBOL program, the Work Area will be filled with the first several lines of the program. By default, the Work Area margins are set at position 7 on the left and position 73 on the right to correspond to the area in which the majority of COBOL statements are placed. However, the cursor control keys may be used to access positions 1 through 7 or 73 through 80.

```
Edit-SAMPLE————165-lines——Line-1———Col-8————Wrap-Ins-Caps-Num-Scroll
F1=help F2=library F3=load-file F4=save-file F5=split-line F6=join-line F7=print
        F9=untype-word-left F10=delete-word-right                       Escape
```

} *Alt Menu Lines*

Figure 4.2 *Control Area of Editor with Alternate Menu displayed.*

The Control Area of the Editor screen is composed of the bottom four lines on the display. The first line in this area is called the Information Line. It contains the name of the file being edited as well as the line and column numbers of the current cursor location. On the right side of this line are status indicators for word-wrap, Insert mode, Caps Lock, Num Lock, and Scroll mode. These indicators are highlighted when these functions have been activated. (A description of these functions appears later in this chapter.) The next two lines of the Control Area are menu lines. Here are located the options currently available and the keys that may be pressed to invoke them. The first menu that appears after invoking Editor is the Main Menu. Two other menus are also available. Pressing and holding the ALT key displays the Alternate Menu, while pressing and holding the CTRL key displays the Control Menu. Figures 4.2 and 4.3 illustrate the options available on these two menus. The fourth line in the Control Area is called the Message Line and is blank most of the time. The Message Line is used by the system to display information such as error messages and reminders.

```
Edit-SAMPLE————165-lines——Line-1———Col-8————Wrap-Ins-Caps-Num-Scroll
F1=help F2=find F3=block F4=clear F5=margins F6=draw/scrns F7=tags F8=word-wrap
F9=window                                                          Escape
```

} *Ctrl Menu Lines*

Figure 4.3 *Control Area of Editor with Control Menu displayed.*

Exiting Personal COBOL

Personal COBOL may be exited by pressing the ESC key. "Exit from Personal COBOL? Y/N" will appear on the Message Line. Enter **Y** to exit or **N** to cancel the exit process. If you attempt to exit Personal COBOL and have not saved the most current version of your work, a reminder message is displayed on the Message Line. The ESC key is also used to quit any function within Personal COBOL as well as to back up through its menu structure.

File Loading and Saving

To load a file into the Work Area of the Editor, the Alternate Menu is used. Pressing [ALT] + [F3] will result in a message asking for the name of the file. The area used to enter the filename contains the current path. If a different path is desired, it may be changed by using the Backspace key to erase the existing path, followed by entering the desired path and filename. If the filename is unknown, press the [F2] key to display a list of the files in the directory. The desired file may be identified by highlighting its name in the list using the [↑] or [↓] arrow keys. Pressing the [ENTER] key twice results in the selected file being loaded into the Work Area.

A file is saved by also using the Alternate Menu. Pressing [ALT] + [F4] results in a similar prompt to that used for loading a file. If the path and filename displayed are not the ones desired, use the Backspace key to erase them and then key in the revision. If a file extension is not specified, the system will use its default of `.CBL`. Pressing the [ENTER] key results in the file being saved.

Typical Mode Settings

Most COBOL programmers enter their programs using uppercase letters, even though Personal COBOL is not case sensitive. Press the [CAPS LOCK] key to toggle between uppercase and lowercase entry modes.

The word-wrap mode is usually turned on. With this function activated, if a word is entered that does not fit on the line, the entire word is automatically moved to begin on the next line. If the word-wrap mode is turned off, the word is split between two lines. The [F8] key on the Control Menu toggles this mode on and off. The default for the word-wrap mode is on.

The Num Lock mode is toggled on and off using the [NUM LOCK] key. It is usually turned off so that the [HOME], [END], [PG UP], and [PG DN] keys on the key pad may be used instead of the numbers that are also on the key pad.

Pressing the [INS] key toggles between the insert and typeover modes of text entry. Turning the insert mode on changes the shape of the cursor as well as highlights the `Ins` status indicator on the Information Line. The insert mode is used during most operations. The typeover mode is generally used when making modifications to portions of a program.

The Scroll mode is toggled on and off with the [SCROLL LOCK] key. It is usually left off. When it is on, pressing an [↑] or [↓] arrow key results in the cursor remaining in place while the lines of text move up or down the screen. When the scroll mode is off, pressing an [↑] or [↓] arrow key results in the cursor moving up or down the screen while the lines of text remain stationary.

Moving the Cursor

To enter and modify COBOL statements throughout a program, the cursor must be moved from one location to another within the source code to make changes or corrections. Horizontal cursor positioning may be accomplished with several keys. The [←] and [→] arrow keys may be used to move the cursor left and right without disturbing existing text. The default tab stopsin Personal COBOL are set at four-position intervals. The Tab ([TAB]) and [SHIFT] + [TAB] (Backtab) keys may be used to move the cursor to the next tab stop on the right or left. If the insert mode is on, pressing the [TAB] key inserts spaces in the positions between the cursor position and the next tab stop. The [END] key may be used to move the cursor to the position after the last character on the line. The [HOME] key may be used to move the cursor to the position next to the left margin.

Vertical positioning of the cursor may be accomplished with several keys. The line the cursor is on is highlighted in the Work Area and is referred to as the current line. The [↑] and [↓] arrow keys may be used to scroll up and down through the lines of text. The [PG UP] and [PG DN] keys may be used to view the previous or following page of text not currently visible on the screen (a page is equal to the number of lines that will fit in the Work Area). Pressing [CTRL] + [PG UP] or [CTRL] + [PG DN] will result in moving the cursor 200 lines up or down. Pressing the [CTRL] + [HOME] or [CTRL] + [END] keys will result in the cursor moving to the first or last line in the file.

Inserting Characters and Lines

The insertion of additional text into a file is generally done with the insert mode turned on. Position the cursor at the place where the new text is to begin and it may be entered at that point. As each new character is keyed, the existing text is moved to the right. Pressing the [ENTER] key with the insert mode turned on results in all text from the cursor to the end of the line being moved to the next line.

Sometimes one or more new lines need to be added to a program. This may be done by inserting blank lines into the file and then keying the new statements on to them. A blank line may be inserted below the current line by placing the cursor at the end of the line and pressing the [ENTER] key. A blank line appears and the cursor is moved to the beginning of this new line. A blank line may be inserted above the current line by placing the cursor at the beginning of the line and pressing the [ENTER] key. In this case, a blank line will be inserted above the current line, but the cursor will remain on the current line. The fastest way to insert one or more blank lines above the current line is to press the [F3] key when the Main Menu is displayed. The cursor may be anywhere on the current line. When the [F3] key is pressed, the existing text moves down one line and the cursor is positioned at the beginning of the inserted new line.

Deleting and Restoring Characters and Lines

Three different keys may be used to delete characters from a line. With the insert mode off, the [SPACE] key may be used to replace any character with a blank. The [DEL] key may be used to erase the character at the cursor position and move the remaining text one position to the left. The Backspace key behaves differently depending on the insert mode. With the insert mode off, pressing the Backspace key results in the character to the left of the cursor being erased and the remaining text being moved left one position. With the insert mode on, pressing the Backspace key erases the character to the left of the cursor but restores any characters that were previously typed over. An entire line of text may be deleted by placing the cursor on the line and using the [F4] key on the Main Menu. The current line is deleted and the lines below are moved up one line.

Any lines deleted within an editing session are saved in a buffer area. The F6 key on the Main Menu may be used to retrieve deleted lines from this buffer. The retrieved line is placed above the current line and removed from the buffer. Lines are restored in reverse order of their deletion. In other words, the last line to be deleted is the first that may be restored.

Moving and Copying Lines

A common technique used to move a single line from one place in the file to another is to delete it with the F4 key, move the cursor to the line below where it is to be moved, and then press the F6 key to restore it. A single line may also be copied using the F5 key on the Main Menu to repeat a line. The current line is duplicated and placed above the current line.

```
Block——————————166-lines——Line-5————Col-8—————Wrap-Ins-Caps-Num-Scroll
F1=help F2=edit-block F3=insert-block F4=define-block   F6=restore-block Escape
```

Figure 4.4 *The Block Menu that appears by pressing* CTRL + F3. *Marking a block begins by placing the cursor on the first line to be included in the block and then pressing* F4.

Blocks of several lines may also be moved and copied. This is accomplished using the Block function of Personal COBOL that is accessed by pressing CTRL + F3 to display the Block Menu. This menu is illustrated in Figure 4.4. Using the Block function begins by identifying the block of lines to be moved or copied. This is done by placing the cursor on the first line of text to be included in the block and then pressing the F4 key. This will cause the Block Submenu to be displayed. The cursor movement keys may then be used to move the cursor down through the lines of text. The lines are highlighted as this is done to mark the ones being included in the block. Figure 4.5 illustrates the Block Submenu and a highlighted portion of the sample program.

```
SAMPLE.CBL
           END-IF.

       21-PRINT-REPORT-HEADING.
           MOVE TITLE-LINE                 TO PRINT-AREA
           WRITE PRINT-RECORD AFTER ADVANCING PAGE
           MOVE +7                         TO LINE-COUNT
           ADD  +1                         TO PAGE-COUNT
           MOVE PAGE-COUNT                 TO RPT-PAGE-NO
           MOVE SUBTITLE-LINE              TO PRINT-AREA
           MOVE 2                          TO REQD
           PERFORM 211-PRINT-REPORT-LINE
           MOVE COLUMN-HEADING-LINE        TO PRINT-AREA
           MOVE 3                          TO REQD
           PERFORM 211-PRINT-REPORT-LINE.

       211-PRINT-REPORT-LINE.
           WRITE PRINT-RECORD AFTER ADVANCING REQD LINES
           ADD REQD                        TO LINE-COUNT.
     /
Block——————————166-lines——Line-127——Col-8—————Wrap-Ins-Caps-Num-Scroll
F1=help F2=find F3=copy-to-block F4=remove-to-block Escape

cursor movement extends marked text
```

Figure 4.5 *A marked block of lines in the sample program. The cursor is moved to adjust the extent of the block.* F3 *or* F4 *may be pressed to either copy the block or remove the block and place it into a buffer area.*

When all of the lines to be included in the block are marked, they may be either moved or copied. To move the block, press the [F4] key to remove the block of lines and place it into a buffer area. At this point, the highlighted block is deleted from the screen and the Block Submenu is replaced with the Block Menu. Place the cursor on the line just above where the block is to be moved and press the [F3] key to insert the block below the current line. To copy a marked block, press the [F3] key to copy the block of lines into the buffer. Place the cursor on the line just above where the block is to be copied and press the [F3] key to insert the block below the current line. The Block menu may be exited by pressing the [ESC] key.

Finding and Replacing

Sometimes there is a need to modify some or all of the occurrences of an item in a COBOL program. The Find Menu of the Editor may be used to locate the occurrences of a text string and, optionally, replace them with a different text string. The Find Menu is accessed by pressing [CTRL] + [F2]. Figure 4.6 illustrates the Find Menu.

```
Find————————stp-166-lines———Line-5————Col-8—————Wrap-Ins-Caps-Num-Scroll
F1=help F3=cursor→Find F4=clear F5=punc F6=case F9=repl-mode(step,all)
Find                                     Replace
```

Text to find is entered here

Text used to replace found text may be entered here.

Figure 4.6 *The Find Menu that appears by pressing* [CTRL] + [F2].

When the Find Menu is invoked, the cursor is placed in the lower-left portion of the Control Area next to the word Find. This is called the Find Buffer. Type the text string to be found into the Find Buffer. Then press the [F2] key to set the contents of the Find Buffer and to position the cursor to the right next to the word Replace. This is called the Replace Bufferand may be used to enter a string to replace the string in the Find Buffer. Pressing [F2] sets the contents of the Replace Buffer and moves the cursor back to the Find Buffer. The [F2] key may be used to cycle back and forth between these two buffers to make changes to their contents. Pressing [CTRL] + [F4] will clear the contents of the current buffer.

Once the Find and Replace Buffer contents are set, the find and replace operation may begin. The cursor is usually placed at the beginning of the file to simplify the searching process. Press the [F10] key to begin a forward search from the cursor to the end of the file to find text equal to that in the Find Buffer. Use the [F9] key for a backward search from the cursor to the beginning of the file. When a matching occurrence is found, a message appears on the Message Line indicating either to press [F8] to replace the occurrence with the contents of the Replace Buffer or to press [F10] to leave the occurrence unchanged and continue the search ([F7] and [F9] for backward searches). This process is repeated until a message appears indicating that all occurrences have been located. The default is for the matching process to ignore the case of any alphabetic characters in text strings. If an exact match on uppercase and lowercase is desired, press [CTRL] + [F6] before initiating the forward or backward search.

Accessing On-line Help

One of the components of Personal COBOL is the On-line Help System (HYHELP). It may be used to view on-screen help information about any tool of the Personal COBOL System. This feature may be accessed at any time by pressing the F1 key to get context-sensitive help. Appropriate help information about the tool in current use is then displayed on the screen. A full explanation of the help facility may be found in Chapter 8 of the *Programmer's Guide*.

Accessing COBOL Syntax Diagrams

Personal COBOL includes an On-line Language Reference component that may be useful for developing COBOL statements. COBOL syntax requirements and options are presented on the screen using syntax diagrams like the one illustrated in Figure 4.7. When editing a program, this

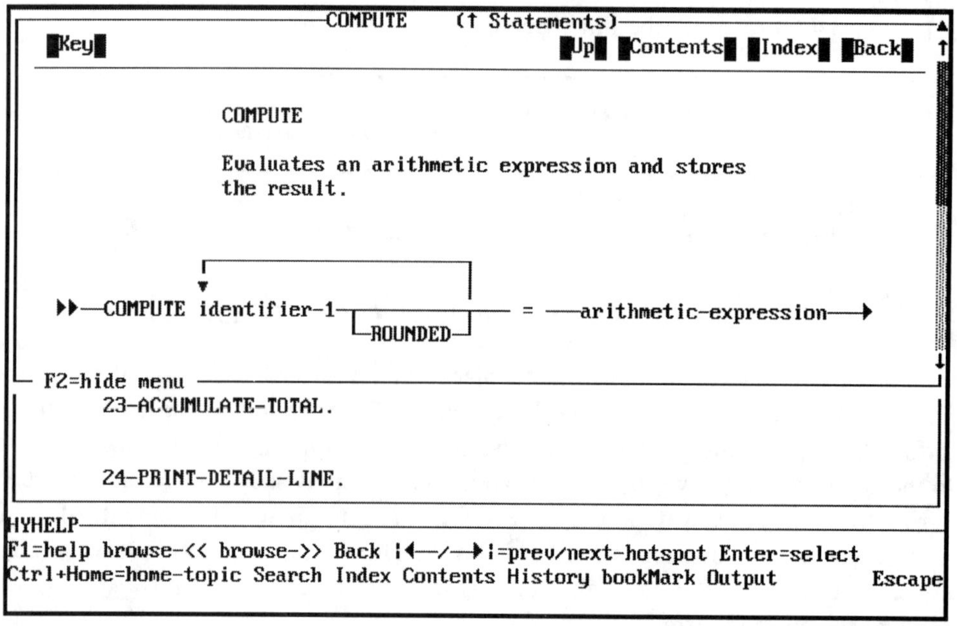

Figure 4.7 *The Syntax Diagram that appears when the cursor is placed on the word "Compute" and* ALT + F1 *is pressed.*

type of information may be accessed by placing the cursor on a COBOL word of interest and pressing ALT + F1. The On-line Reference function will then display either the function of the word with a syntax diagram or a table of contents from which a topic may be selected. A complete explanation of the Language Reference function and syntax diagrams may be found in Chapter 9 of the *Programmer's Guide*.

Chapter 5

Compiling COBOL Programs

The Compilation Process

After a COBOL source code file has been created and saved using Editor, the compilation process may begin. There are two primary purposes of this process. The first is to locate and fix any COBOL syntax errors that may be in the source code statements. The second is to translate error-free COBOL source code into object code that may be executed on the computer used to process data in the manner intended by the program.

The compilation process has three basic phases. First, the compiler is invoked and the source code file is made available to it. Second, the compiler reads through all of the COBOL statements checking them for syntax errors and creates an output listing of the source code. If syntax errors are found, messages are included in the output listing indicating the location, severity, and type of each error. Third, if no severe errors are found, an object code file is created. If severe errors are found, they must be corrected using Editor and the compilation process must be repeated. (Error severity is explained later in this chapter.)

It is quite common for a program to contain syntax errors when the compiler makes its first attempt to compile a program. The number of errors found is typically a factor of how much experience the programmer has in writing COBOL statements. Even very experienced COBOL programmers make keying errors and other minor mistakes. Beginning COBOL programmers tend to make lots of errors at first because they are not yet familiar with the language.

Invoking the COBOL Compiler

The compiler component of the Personal COBOL System is called Checker. Before attempting to invoke Checker, the source code file must be loaded into Editor. If any changes have been made to the source code, it must also be saved before attempting to invoke Checker.

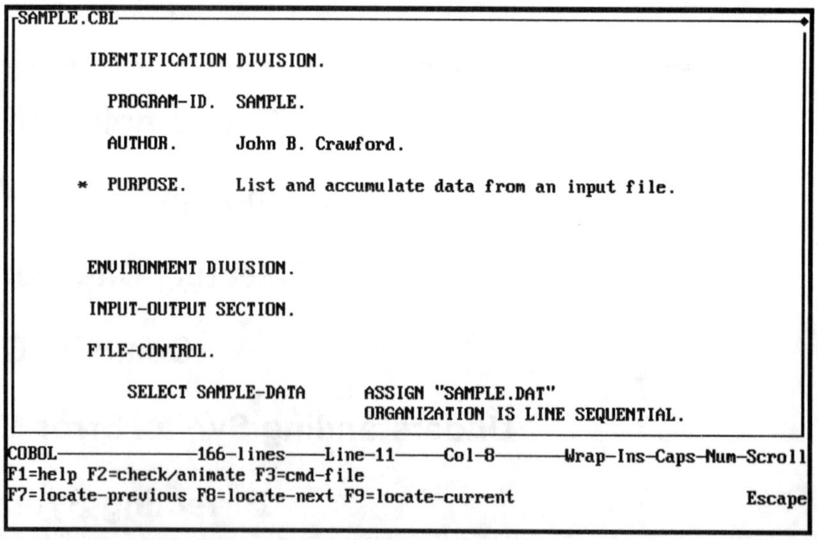

Figure 5.1 *The COBOL Menu that appears after pressing* F2 *on the Editor Main Menu.*

The process of invoking Checker is begun by pressing the F2 key on the Editor Main Menu. This results in the COBOL Menu being displayed, as illustrated in Figure 5.1. Pressing F2 again results in the Checker Menu being displayed, as illustrated in Figure 5.2. Pressing the Enter key at this point will invoke Checker and it will begin to check the program for syntax errors. However, before doing this, there are some options shown on the Checker Menu that may need to be selected to control how Checker behaves.

Indicates that Checker will pause after each error it finds

Indicates that Checker will display errors on the monitor.

```
Checker-Check———Pause-List-Con——————————————————————————————————————
F1=help F2=check/anim F3=pause F4=list                  F7=ref      Esc
F9/F10=directives       check SAMPLE                           ↵
```

Figure 5.2 *The Checker Menu that appears after pressing F2 on the COBOL Menu.*

Selecting Checker Options

As Checker reads through the source code file checking for syntax errors, it displays the lines of source code on the screen. Checker has a pause option that may be toggled on and off by pressing the F3 key. The default is on, as indicated by the word Pause on the Information Line (shown in Figure 5.2). When the pause feature is on, Checker pauses each time a syntax error is found in the source code. Checking is suspended, an error message is displayed, and a prompt appears asking how the user wishes to proceed, as illustrated in Figure 5.3. Entering **Y** directs Checker to continue with its checking process and to pause again if another error is found. Entering **N** terminates the checking process followed by the display of the Editor screen. Entering **Z** directs Checker to enter the zoom mode and continue its checking process without further pauses. When the pause option is off, Checker does not pause and display a message when it finds a syntax error.

The List option is used to specify how Checker should report the results of its checking process. There are four options: List-Con, Print, List-File, and Nolist. Pressing the F4 key repeatedly cycles through these options, displaying the active one on the Information Line. The default is List-Con (shown in Figure 5.2). This option directs Checker to place its output listing on the monitor (console). This is the option most frequently used and is chosen when not too many errors are expected to be found in the checking process. The Print option directs Checker to produce its output listing on the printer as it conducts its checking process. The List-File option directs Checker to place its output listing into a file. The default filename used for this is the name of the source code file with an extension of **.LST**. The Print or List-File options are usually selected when a lot of errors are expected, such as when a novice programmer is compiling a program for the first or second time where there may be a need to see large blocks of code to facilitate making corrections. The Print option is rather slow. The List-File option is faster, but the resulting **.LST** file must be printed either by using the DOS PRINT command or by loading it into Editor and using the F7 key to invoke its Print option. The List-File option is also used when the program has been completed (tested successfully) and final documentation is needed. The Nolist option directs Checker to not create an output listing. This option would be selected only when a new output listing is not required, such as when the object code file was somehow lost and is being recreated.

The Ref option may be used to request that additional reference information be placed in the output listing. There are two types of additional reference information. One is called REF and, when selected, results in the output listing including the object code memory addresses of each data item and command. This is usually not needed. The other option is called XREF and can be very useful information during program testing. When selected, Checker adds cross reference information at the end of the output listing that identifies all of the items described in the DATA DIVISION and procedures in the PROCEDURE DIVISION. Some of the information it gives about each of these includes:

- its name and type
- the line number where it was defined
- the line numbers of instructions referring to it
- the number of times it appears in the program

A complete discussion of the cross-reference listing is beyond the scope of this manual. However, this option is often selected when program testing is about to begin as well as when creating final program documentation. Pressing the F7 key cycles through the four possible combinations of selecting these two options. The default is for neither to be selected. The other three possibilities are REF, XREF, and REF+XREF.

Compiler Directives

There are also several other directives that may be given to Checker. The ones discussed above are the ones that sometimes need to be varied. The remaining directives have defaults that work well most of the time. A complete explanation of all directives may be found in Chapter 13 of the *Programmer's Guide*. Additional directives may be selected by pressing the F10 key on the Checker Menu. After making these selections, the F9 key on the Checker Menu is used to toggle between making them active or inactive.

Understanding Syntax Error Messages

COBOL programs are made up of reserved words that the compiler recognizes as well as programmer-supplied identifiers that must be composed using specific rules. These reserved words and identifiers are used to formulate COBOL statements, the majority of which are used either to describe data or to specify how data are to be processed. When a COBOL source code file contains a statement that does not conform to the patterns recognized by Checker, an error message is produced. Figure 5.3 illustrates the format that Checker uses to report the syntax errors it finds.

Two lines are placed under the statement containing the error. The first line contains a number followed by a letter. In Figure 5.3, there is a "12" followed by an "S" and a string of asterisks. Each error message has been assigned a unique number to identify it and to serve as an aid for

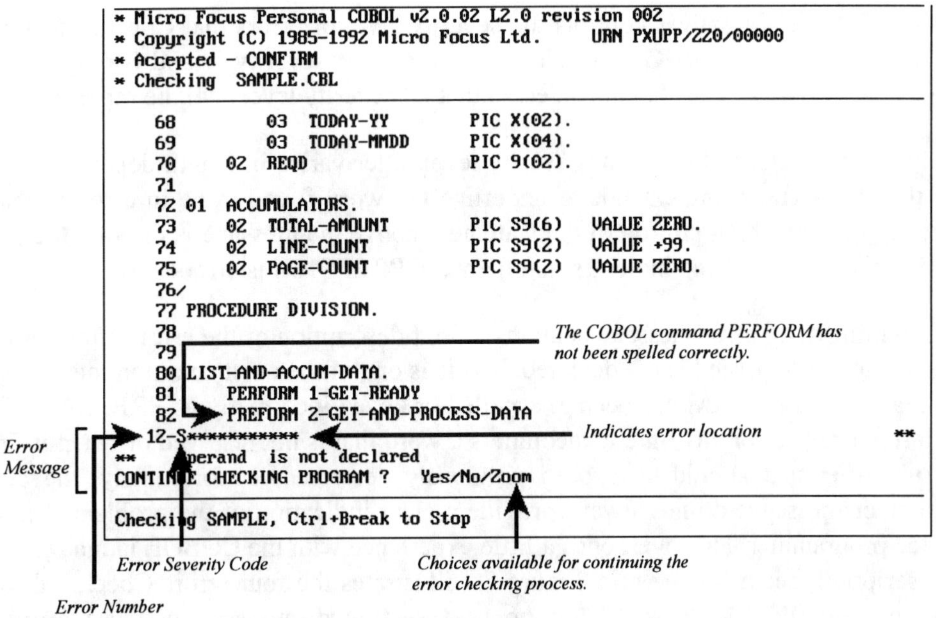

Figure 5.3 *Typical display that appears when Checker finds an error.*

finding it in reference materials. There are several hundred different messages that may be issued by Checker. Unfortunately, they are not documented in the *Programmer's Guide*. However, they are documented in the On-line Reference. The letter following the error message number is an indicator of how severe the error is. There are five different letters used for this purpose. In descending order of severity, they are:

U = Unrecoverable—an error that has forced Checker to stop checking. This is usually a system error rather than a COBOL syntax error, such as a disk failure occurring during compilation.

S = Severe—a statement has been found that does not conform to the rules for writing COBOL statements. This is the most common type of error. Object code will not be produced from a source code file containing severe errors. After Checker finds a severe error, it ignores remaining source code until it can continue checking at the next word it recognizes or the beginning of the next statement. As a result, there may be errors in the ignored source code that are not reported.

E = Error—an error was found that Checker can try to correct. It makes assumptions about what was intended and produces object code based on those assumptions.

W = Warning—a potential error or inconsistency was found that Checker assumes is correct, but the statement should be checked by the programmer.

I = Information—something was found in the source code to which Checker wishes to draw the programmer's attention.

One of the COBOL Directives controls the severity level of errors that Checker will report. The default directive is WARNING 1 which reports errors of severity U and S only. Changing the directive to WARNING 3 is recommended so that all severity levels will be reported.

The string of asterisks following the severity level letter varies in length depending on the location of the error. The string extends to underline the word found to be in error so that the programmer can know which portion of the statement above the message is causing the problem. In Figure 5.3, the asterisk string indicates that the word PREFORM is erroneous.

The second line of an error message contains a brief description of the error found. In Figure 5.3, this description is "Operand is not declared." This is one of the most common messages reported. In this example, PERFORM has been misspelled or keyed incorrectly as PREFORM. Checker is likely to report this error any time it encounters a word that is not reserved or when it finds an unknown identifier that should have been previously described. Unfortunately, the descriptions given in error messages do not always provide a clear indication of the problem, particularly to the novice programmer. However, once a little experience with the COBOL language is obtained, these descriptions seem less cryptic. Figure 5.4 illustrates the four errors Checker discovered in the source code file **SAMPLE.CBL**. The next section discusses how these errors may be corrected.

```
* Micro Focus Personal COBOL v2.0.02 L2.0 revision 002
* Copyright (C) 1985-1992 Micro Focus Ltd.      URN PXUPP/ZZ0/00000
* Accepted - CONFIRM
* Checking  SAMPLE.CBL
    82      PREFORM 2-GET-AND-PROCESS-DATA             ]  First error found    **
*   12-S***********
**      Operand  is not declared
    138      ADD IN-AMOUNT                 TO TOTAL-AMOUNT.  ]  Second error found   **
*   12-S*****************
**      Operand  is not declared
    142      MOVE IN-AMOUNT                TO RPT-AMOUNT   ]  Third error found    **
*   12-S******************
**      Operand  is not declared

    162
    163
    164****** END OF SAMPLE PROGRAM SOURCE CODE ******
    165
    166
*        3-FINISH                                      ]  Fourth error found   **
* 348-S********
**      Procedure name 3-FINISH undeclared
CONTINUE CHECKING PROGRAM ?   Yes/No/Zoom

Checking SAMPLE, Ctrl+Break to Stop
```

Figure 5.4 *The messages displayed by Checker for the four errors it found in the sample program.*

Correcting Syntax Errors

The Personal COBOL System provides some handy features for making corrections to syntax errors. When Checker finishes its checking process, control is automatically returned to Editor. Displayed at the top of the Work Area is the first statement Checker found to be in error. The line is highlighted and the cursor is placed under the word that caused the error to be reported. Figure 5.5 shows how the screen appeared immediately after Checker finished processing the **SAMPLE.CBL** source code file. Notice that the error description has been displayed on the Message Line at the bottom of the screen. At this point, the word PREFORM may be edited to change it to the correct word PERFORM.

```
SAMPLE.CBL
           PREFORM 2-GET-AND-PROCESS-DATA
               UNTIL END-OF-FILE = "TRUE "
           PERFORM 3-FINISH-UP
           STOP RUN.


       1-GET-READY.
           PERFORM 11-SETUP-RPT-DATE-AND-MARGIN
           PERFORM 12-OPEN-FILES.

       11-SETUP-RPT-DATE-AND-MARGIN.
           ACCEPT TODAYS-DATE-HOLD       FROM DATE
           MOVE TODAY-MMDD               TO RPT-MMDD
           MOVE TODAY-YY                 TO RPT-YY
           MOVE SPACES                   TO LEFT-MARGIN.

       12-OPEN-FILES.
           OPEN INPUT  SAMPLE-DATA

Edit-SAMPLE———166-lines——Line-82——Col-18———Wrap-Ins-Caps-Num-Scroll
F1=help F2=COBOL F3=insert-line F4=delete-line F5=repeat-line F6=restore-line
F7=retype-char F8=restore-char F9=word-left F10=word-right      Alt Ctrl Escape
 *  12 Operand  is not declared
```

Line upon which the first error is located. The command PERFORM has been misspelled.

Description of error

Figure 5.5 *Display that appears just after Checker completed its syntax checking process. The Editor is active so that errors may be corrected.*

The next error found in the source code by Checker may be located with another special feature of Personal COBOL. Pressing [F2] on the Main Menu to display the COBOL Menu and then pressing [F8] results in the screen shown in Figure 5.6. The source code line reported in the second of Checker's error messages is at the top of the screen. Notice that there are three choices on the second line of the COBOL Menu: [F7]=locate-previous, [F8]=locate-next, and [F9]=locate-current.

The [F7] and [F8] keys may be used to jump backward or forward through the source code file to edit the lines reported as having errors. It is also possible to use the standard cursor movement keys to move around to any desired portion of the program. If this is done, the [F9] key may be used to return to the line with the most recently displayed error.

The second and third errors found in the sample program serve to illustrate an important point in understanding and correcting syntax errors. It is not uncommon for the compiler to report an error on a line that may not need changing to solve the problem. Notice in Figure 5.4 that IN-AMOUNT has been flagged on two different lines of source code as being in error. However, these lines of code may be exactly what the programmer wanted. These two errors were reported by Checker because IN-AMOUNT was not previously described in the DATA DIVISION of the program and, therefore, was not recognized during the check of the statements in the PROCEDURE DIVISION. Figure 5.7 shows that IN-AMT was described in the DATA DIVISION, not IN-AMOUNT. In this example, the second and third errors may be corrected by changing just

```
SAMPLE.CBL
         ADD IN-AMOUNT                   TO TOTAL-AMOUNT.

     24-PRINT-DETAIL-LINE.
         MOVE IN-NAME                    TO RPT-NAME
         MOVE IN-AMOUNT                  TO RPT-AMOUNT
         MOVE DETAIL-LINE                TO PRINT-AREA
         PERFORM 211-PRINT-REPORT-LINE
         MOVE 2                          TO REQD.


     3-FINISH-UP.
         PERFORM 31-PRINT-TOTAL-LINE
         PERFORM 32-CLOSE-FILES.

     31-PRINT-TOTAL-LINE.
         MOVE TOTAL-AMOUNT               TO RPT-TOTAL
         MOVE TOTAL-LINE                 TO PRINT-AREA
         MOVE 3                          TO REQD
COBOL-------------166-lines---Line-138---Col-24-----Wrap-Ins-Caps-Num-Scroll
F1=help F2=check/animate F3=cmd-file
F7=locate-previous F8=locate-next F9=locate-current                   Escape
 * 12 Operand  is not declared
```

Line upon which the second error is located. The word IN-AMOUNT does not match any identifiers described in the DATA DIVISION.

Options available to move cursor from one error to another.

Figure 5.6 *Display that appears after pressing [F2] on the Main Menu to get the COBOL Menu, then pressing [F8] to locate the second error found by the Checker.*

one line instead of two—editing IN-AMT to IN-AMOUNT. This would be done by using the cursor movement keys to move up to line 31, make the change, and then using the [F9] key to return to line 130 where the second error was reported. The correction process could then be continued from this point.

```
SAMPLE.CBL
       FD  SAMPLE-DATA.
       01  INPUT-RECORD.
           02  IN-NAME                  PIC X(20).
           02  IN-AMT                   PIC 9(04).

       FD  SAMPLE-REPORT.
       01  PRINT-RECORD.
           02  LEFT-MARGIN              PIC X(20).
           02  PRINT-AREA               PIC X(40).


       WORKING-STORAGE SECTION.

       01  REPORT-LINES.
           02  TITLE-LINE               PIC X(40)
               VALUE "                    SAMPLE REPORT                  ".
           02  SUBTITLE-LINE.
               03  REPORT-DATE.
                   04  RPT-MMDD         PIC XX/XX/.
```

This field has been described with IN-AMT as its identifier, not IN-AMOUNT.

Figure 5.7 *A portion of the DATA DIVISION displayed in the Work Area showing how the fields in the input data file are described.*

Another common error to deal with is one like the fourth error reported by Checker when it checked the sample source code. Figure 5.4 shows this error message to be reported at the end of the source code listing. It is described as "Procedure name 3-FINISH undeclared." Typically, this message appears whenever a PERFORM statement refers to a Paragraph Name that does not exist in the Procedure Division. Notice in Figure 5.5 that the third line from the top contains PERFORM 3-FINISH. This is the statement that caused the error to be reported, but Checker did not know there was a problem until it had finished checking all of the statements in the program without finding a paragraph named 3-FINISH. Nor was any line number given indicating the location of the unrecognized procedure name. Now notice in Figure 5.6 that there is a Paragraph Name near the center of the screen that is named 3-FINISH-UP. This problem may be corrected only by making the statements consistent. In other words, either the PERFORM 3-FINISH statement must be changed to read PERFORM 3-FINISH-UP or the Paragraph Name must be changed from 3-FINISH-UP to read 3-FINISH. The inconsistent use of data and procedure names is probably the most common syntax error made and many times the line flagged as being in error is not the one needing to be changed. Other common syntax errors include failing to put a period at the end of a paragraph or after a paragraph name, omitting a hyphen in the middle of an identifier, using a reserved word as an identifier, and omitting a needed section name. Again, experience in COBOL programming tends to reduce the likelihood of these types of errors.

After each time Checker is used, as many errors as possible should be corrected before activating Checker again. Also, *the new version of the program must be saved prior to each activation of Checker*. Once all errors are corrected and Checker has produced an object code file, program testing may begin.

Object Code Produced by Checker

When no severe errors are found by Checker, it produces a file containing what is referred to in the Personal COBOL System as intermediate code. This file contains compact, binary pseudo-code that is machine independent. The Run Time and Animator components of the Personal COBOL System interpret the intermediate code during execution so that the program runs on the PC under DOS. The intermediate code file is given a filename equal to the source code filename, but with the extension .INT. For example, the intermediate code file produced by Checker in the sample program is **`SAMPLE.INT`**.

The generation of intermediate code, instead of machine language, makes it possible for Micro Focus to have a more versatile software product that may be used to produce programs with COBOL that will run on a variety of different computers using different operating systems. Since the intermediate code is interpreted during program execution by the runtime module, having different runtime modules tailored for different operating environments is all that is required to execute the same program in any of those environments.

Chapter 6

Developing Test Data Files

Program Testing

Input Data Files

Sequential Files

Line Sequential Files

Setting Up Editor to Create a Test Data File

Entering The Data

Program Testing

The testing phase of the program development process is a critical step. After all syntax errors have been corrected, it is very important that a program be thoroughly tested to insure that it works as intended. To accomplish this, the program should be executed under conditions that duplicate its future operating environment as closely as possible. An important part of the testing process, therefore, is to execute the program using input data files that are representative of the actual data the program will have to process when it becomes fully operational. This requires that considerable planning be done so that the files to be used for testing contain all of the various combinations of data values that might be encountered during future use of the program.

Input Data Files

It is very important that the COBOL program to be tested contains the record description that exactly matches the way the records in the test data file have been designed. A common error is to design a test data file using the PICTURE clauses in the COBOL program to determine how the test file records should be created. But the test file must be designed to match the design of the file that is actually going to be used when the program becomes operational. If the description of the record in the COBOL program is not correct, designing the test data records using that description will result in a poorly tested program that will not execute properly when placed into production.

The data used by computer programs to perform required processing may originate from a variety of sources. Some data may be entered via a keyboard interactively as the program executes. Other data may be provided to the program by a database management system. However, a significant number of programs get their data by directly accessing files that reside on the computer's disk drives.

Data stored in files may be organized in several different ways. The organization methods used most for business information systems are sequential, indexed, and relative file organizations. The development of test data files that use indexed or relative organization usually requires that a special program be written to create them. However, sequential files may be created using a text editing program such as Editor of the Personal COBOL System.

Sequential Files

Sequential files are the simplest type of file organization. The records that form the file are placed in the file one at a time in the order they are written. Typically, these records are all the same length, each one being composed of one or more fields.

The fields making up the records of a sequential file must be consistent in both position and length. For example, if one of the fields making up the records is a name field, even though the values in this field may vary in length, it must begin in the same position in each record and be composed of the exact same number of characters. This is done by designing the field to be long enough to contain the longest name likely to be processed. Names with fewer characters are padded on the right side with spaces. Similarly, numeric fields must be consistent from record to record. Numeric fields must be designed to be long enough to contain the highest value likely to be processed. Values that do not require all of the positions allocated to the field are padded with leading zeroes. It is critical that test data file records be composed of fields that are consistent in position and length because COBOL programs depend on this in the way they locate data for processing.

Figure 6.1 illustrates the characteristics of the sequential file used to test the sample program referred to in this manual. It is a very simple sequential file with only two fields per record, a name field and an amount field. Notice that the name field always begins in position one and the amount field always begins in position twenty-one. Also notice that the names that are shorter than twenty characters have been padded on the right side with spaces and the amounts with values under 1000 have been padded with leading zeroes. As a result, each record in this sequential file is the same length and the fields within each record are consistent in position and length.

Position 21

Position 1

```
ADVANCED TECHNOLOGY 3616
BRAVADO SUPPLIERS   1947
COMPLETE EVERYTHING 0175
DELPHI FACTORIES    2011
ECHOTECH, LTD.      8737
FASTER FOREVER      0139
GROOVEY, INC.       4542
HASTEN 2 U          [illegible]89
INNOVATIVE PARTS    6405
JAGS R US           3651
JUMBO INDUSTRIAL    7524
KILOCOMP CORP.      7320
KWIKTECH, INC.      5432
LIMBO COMPONENTS    9734
MACHO MECHANO       6789
NIMBLE AGENTS       9527
OPTIMUM UNLIMITED   2645
PRECISION MFG.      0579
QUICKY IMPORTS      1083
RECLAIMED STUFF     3582
RELIABLE SUPPLY     5177
SECURITY PROVIDERS  2435
SUITABLE SUPPLIER   1827
TECHNIQUE BOUTIQUE  3687
ULTIMATE FACTORS    2482
VERIFIABLE SUPPLY   1623
WASTENOT LIMITED    0040
XEROMATIC CORP.     4914
YOUNGCO, INC.       3253
ZZYZZX TECHNOLOGIES 4524
```

Unused name positions are padded with spaces

Leading zeros are added to amounts under 1000.

Figure 6.1 *List of records in the input data file used to test the sample program.*

Line Sequential Files

Line sequential files are a special type of sequential file. They correspond directly to text files like the ones produced by typical text editing software. A major difference between a standard sequential file and a line sequential file is that the records in a line sequential file have trailing spaces removed causing them to vary in length. Another difference is that each record in a line sequential file ends with a two-position record delimiter composed of a carriage return character followed by a line feed character. These delimiting characters are the ones that are placed in a file when the ENTER key is pressed during text editing. How these records are physically processed varies among different operating systems. *But the key point is that if a sequential test data file is created with Editor or similar text editing software, the COBOL program reading it must contain the ORGANIZATION IS LINE SEQUENTIAL clause in the SELECT statement for the file.*

Setting Up Editor to Create a Test Data File

Using Editor to create a line sequential data file is very similar to using Editor to create a COBOL source code file. The primary difference is that different margin settings must be used. This is because COBOL source statements are generally entered beginning in position eight, while data records almost always begin in position one.

The process begins by invoking Personal COBOL with the PCOBOL command at the DOS prompt and acknowledging the copyright screen by pressing any key. After the Editor Main Menu appears, pressing the CTRL key results in the display shown in Figure 6.2. Notice the

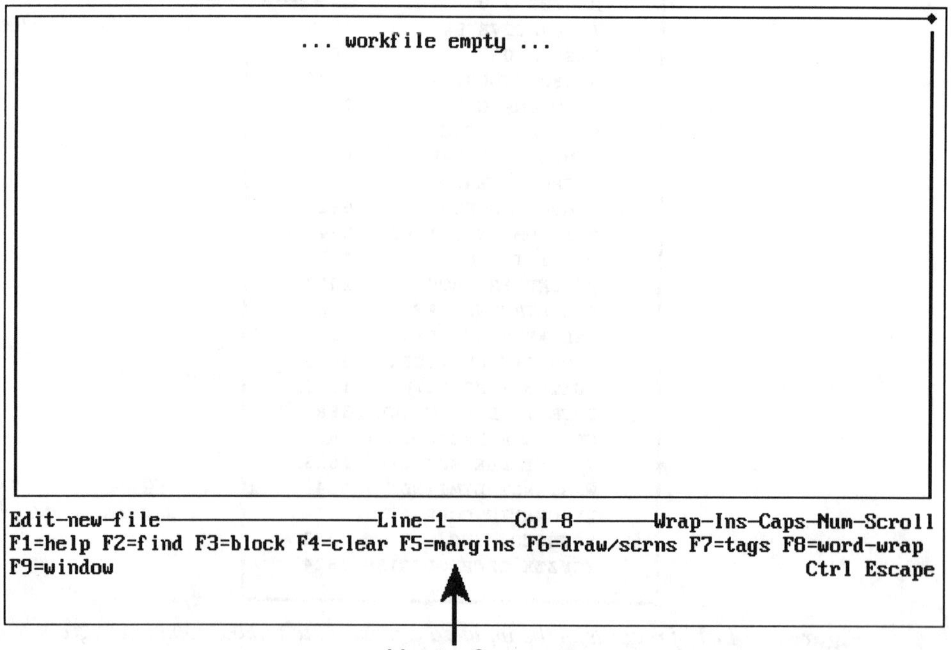

Margins Option

Figure 6.2 *The Control Menu that appears after pressing the* CTRL *key on the Editor's Main Menu.*

F5=margins option. Selecting this option by pressing CTRL + F5 results in the Margins Menu appearing, as illustrated in Figure 6.3. Notice the two vertical bars in the Work Area as well as the Left and Right Margin information shown on the Message Line. This display indicates that the default left margin is set to 7 and the default right margin is set to 73. These defaults are appropriate for entering a COBOL program, but are not likely to be appropriate for entering test data.

Changing the margins to be appropriate for a test data file is quite simple. Almost all data files begin the first field of each record in position one. Therefore, the left margin needs to be set to zero so that the first character entered will be in position one. This may be done in several ways. Pressing the F5 key moves the left vertical bar and the left margin setting one position to the left (out). The left margin may be set to zero, then, by pressing the F5 key repeatedly until the left vertical bar disappears and the left margin setting shown on the Message Line reads zero. However, a faster way to accomplish this is by pressing the F9 key to achieve "fullpage-left."

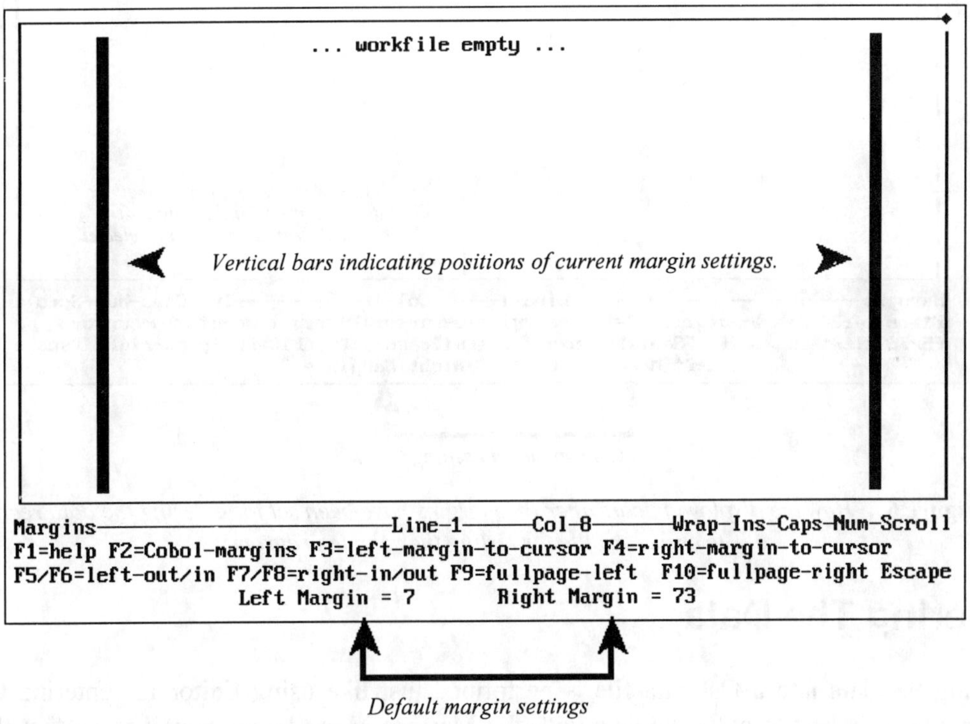

Figure 6.3 *The Margins Menu that appears by pressing* CTRL + F5 *on the Main Menu.*

The right margin must be set so that all of the data needed in the record may be entered. Therefore, the right margin setting must be one position to the right of the last position needed by the rightmost field in the record. For example, the records in the **SAMPLE.DAT** file needed to be 24 characters long so that they could hold a 20-character name followed by a four-digit amount. The right margin, then, needed to be set at position 25, as illustrated in Figure 6.4. The right margin may also be set in several ways. One way is to press the F7 or F8 keys repeatedly to move the right vertical bar to the left (in) or right (out) until it is in the correct position. Another way is to move the cursor to the last position on the line where a character will be entered and then press the [F4] key. This results in the right vertical bar being set one position to the right of the cursor.

One other setting must be made before the test data may be entered. *The word-wrap feature of Editor must be turned off.* This is done by using the [ESC] key to exit the Margins Menu and return to the Control Menu then pressing the [F8] key to turn off word-wrap. Notice in Figure 6.4 that the word Wrap does not appear on the Information Line (as it did in Figure 6.3). If the word-wrap feature of Editor is not disabled, when the last character on the line is entered, the word-wrap feature will move all of the characters entered since the last space down to the beginning of the next line.

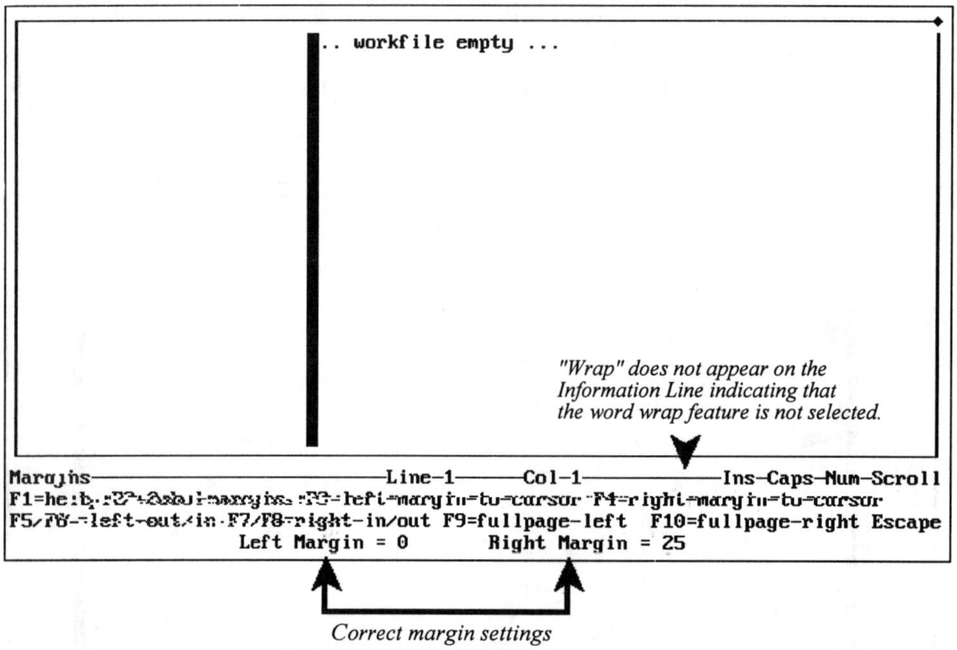

Figure 6.4 *How the display appears after the margins have been set for entering the data records to create the file for testing the sample program.*

Entering The Data

Entering the data into a test data file is performed just like using Editor for entering COBOL statements. It is best to enter the data with the Margins Menu being displayed so that the right vertical bar is visible. Simply place the cursor at the top-left corner of the screen and begin keying in the characters that are supposed to be in the first record of the test data file. As the last character is entered, the cursor will automatically jump down to the beginning of the next line, so the [ENTER] key need not be pressed at the end of each line. Figure 6.5 depicts how the screen looked after the first two records of the **SAMPLE.DAT** file were entered.

Key in the data until all of the planned records have been entered. Figure 6.6 depicts the **SAMPLE.DAT** file after the last record was entered. Once data entry is complete, the file must be given a filename and saved.

```
ADVANCED TECHNOLOGY 3616
BRAVADO SUPPLIES    1947
........................end of text.........................................

Margins————————2-lines————Line-3————Col-1——————————Ins-Caps-Num-Scroll
F1=help F2=Cobol-margins F3=left-margin-to-cursor F4=right-margin-to-cursor
F5/F6=left-out/in F7/F8=right-in/out F9=fullpage-left  F10=fullpage-right Escape
                Left Margin = 0          Right Margin = 25
```

Figure 6.5 *How the display appears after two records are entered.*

It is a common practice to give data files an extension of .DAT. One caution is in order, though, for users of Personal COBOL. *If a file is loaded into Editor that has an extension of .DAT, the left margin defaults to position 0 and the right margin defaults to position 81.* This does not create a serious problem, however. The right margin may be reset to wherever it is needed if additional records are to be added to the file. The margin settings primarily control how Editor behaves during the keying process, not how the records are processed during the saving and retrieving processes.

```
SAMPLE.DAT
KWIKTECH, INC.      5432
LIMBO COMPONENTS    9734
MACHO MECHANO       6789
NIMBLE AGENTS       9527
OPTIMUM UNLIMITED   2645
PRECISION MFG.      0579
QUICKY IMPORTS      1083
RECLAIMED STUFF     3582
RELIABLE SUPPLY     5177
SECURITY PROVIDERS  2435
SUITABLE SUPPLIER   1827
TECHNIQUE BOTIQUE   3687
ULTIMATE FACTORS    2482
VERIFIABLE SUPPLY   1623
WASTENOT LIMITED    0040
XEROMATIC CORP.     4914
YOUNGCO, INC.       3253
ZZYZZX TECHNOLOGIES 4524
........................end of text.........................................

Margins————————30-lines————Line-13————Col-1——————————Ins-Caps-Num-Scroll
F1=help F2=Cobol-margins F3=left-margin-to-cursor F4=right-margin-to-cursor
F5/F6=left-out/in F7/F8=right-in/out F9=fullpage-left  F10=fullpage-right Escape
                Left Margin = 0          Right Margin = 25
```

Figure 6.6 *How display appears after last record is entered. At this point, the* [ESC] *key may be pressed to return to the Main Menu, followed by the* [ALT] + [F4] *keys to save the file.*

Chapter 7

Program Testing with Animator

Program Execution

Testing with PCOBRUN

Testing with Animator

Animating in Step Mode

Animating in Go Mode

Animating in Zoom Mode

Using Breakpoints

Monitoring Data Items during Animation

Encountering Runtime Errors

Exiting Animator

Additional Features of Animator

Program Execution

After Checker has successfully compiled a COBOL source program with no severe errors and the test data files have been created, the program may be executed to find out if it is processing as planned. The Personal COBOL System provides two components that may be used to execute a program: PCOBRUN and Animator.

PCOBRUN is an independent runtime module of the Personal COBOL System used to perform a quick test of a program or to execute a program that has been fully tested and is known to be working properly. However, Animator is the better choice for testing because it contains interactive features that enhance the programmer's ability to locate and correct errors within a program that is processing incorrectly.

Testing with PCOBRUN

PCOBRUN is designed to be used primarily for executing finished programs when they are needed to perform their intended processing. However, PCOBRUN may also be used to execute a program for testing purposes. PCOBOL must be exited before PCOBRUN may be used. It is activated by entering PCOBRUN at the DOS prompt followed by the name of the program. For example, to execute the SAMPLE program, **`PCOBRUN SAMPLE`** would be entered at the DOS prompt. The system would then locate the **`SAMPLE.INT`** file produced by Checker, load it into the computer's memory, and begin executing the program. The output file(s) produced by the program are then inspected to see if they contain the anticipated results based on the test data processed.

Testing with Animator

Animator is the usual choice for program testing. It provides several useful features that greatly enhance the programmer's ability to locate logic errors. Its primary advantage in program testing is that it can provide a step-by-step display of the COBOL instructions on the screen as they are executed. This enables the programmer to monitor the progress of execution while seeing how the source code statements make the computer behave.

Animator is activated from within PCOBOL in a manner similar to the way Checker is activated. Pressing [F2] on the Editor's Main Menu results in the display of the Checker Menu. [F2] may then be used repeatedly to toggle between Check and Animate. Figure 7.1 illustrates how the screen might appear when Animator is about to be selected to execute and test the SAMPLE program. Pressing the [ENTER] key at this point results in the display of the Animator Menu shown in Figure 7.2. Notice that the COBOL statements at the beginning of the PROCEDURE DIVISION of the program are now displayed on the screen and the first executable instruction will be highlighted on your screen. The program is now ready to be executed using one of three different modes: Step, Go, and Zoom. The first letter of each option will be highlighted as well to indicate that pressing that key invokes that option.

```
SAMPLE.CBL

      IDENTIFICATION DIVISION.

        PROGRAM-ID.   SAMPLE.

        AUTHOR.       John B. Crawford.

      * PURPOSE.      List and accumulate data from an input file.


      ENVIRONMENT DIVISION.

      INPUT-OUTPUT SECTION.

      FILE-CONTROL.

          SELECT SAMPLE-DATA      ASSIGN "SAMPLE.DAT"

Checker-Animate           List-File
F1=help F2=check/anim F3=pause F4=list                   F7=ref          Esc
F9/F10=directives       animate SAMPLE
```

[F2] is used to toggle between the Check and Animate functions.

Figure 7.1 *How the display appears after using the [F2] key to toggle to the Animate function of the Checker Menu.*

Animating in Step Mode

The Step mode is used to gain full control over program execution speed. Each time the [S] key is pressed, a COBOL statement is executed and the next instruction is highlighted. The [S] key may be repeatedly pressed as rapidly or slowly as desired. This mode permits the programmer to execute instructions at a speed that makes it easy to determine exactly how the program is behaving. However, using this mode can be slow when executing parts of the program that are not of immediate interest in the testing process.

Animating in Go Mode

The Go mode is used to execute instructions at a constant rate. The rate may be selected by pressing the number keys 0 through 9. The lower the number, the slower the program executes. The higher the number, the faster it executes. The speed that is currently selected is displayed on the Information Line. The default speed is 5. The speed may be changed at any time by pressing a different number and the Go mode may be terminated by pressing the [ESC] key. This mode of execution is most useful when some parts of the program need to be observed closely while others do not. The speed is changed as required to best observe the behavior of various parts of the program.

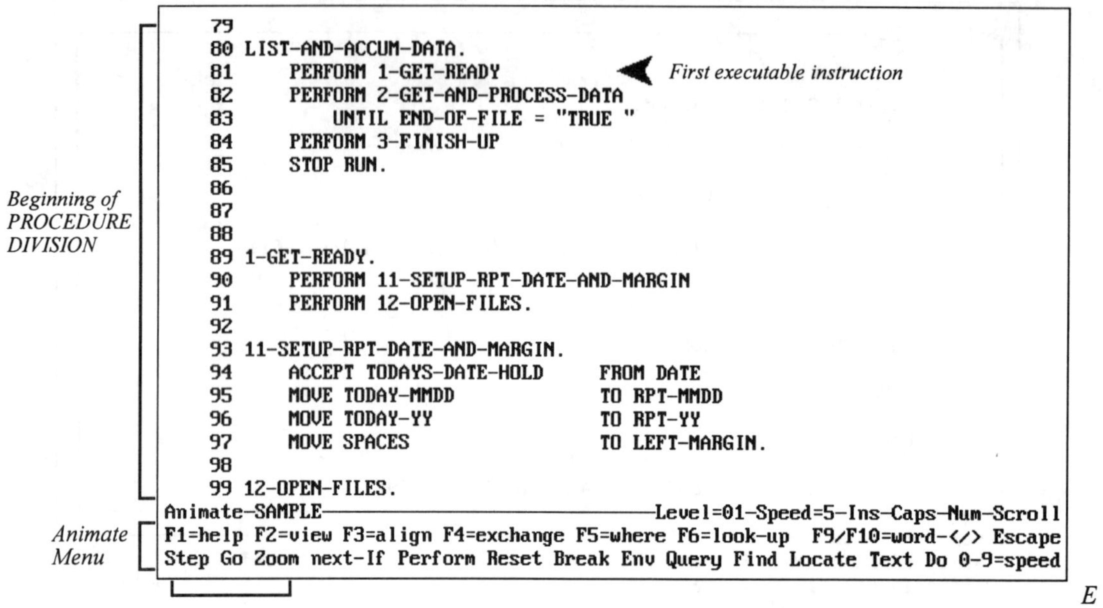

Figure 7.2 *When Animator is invoked, the Work Area is loaded with the beginning lines of the PROCEDURE DIVISION with the first executable instruction highlighted.*

Animating in Zoom Mode

The Zoom mode is used to execute the program very rapidly when no instructions need to be watched as they execute. The Zoom mode of execution is very similar to executing the program with PCOBRUN. The advantage of using this mode over PCOBRUN, however, is that it is not necessary to exit and reenter PCOBOL between each test, change, and recompile. The Zoom mode is most often used during the first and last tests of a program. It is a fast way to first test a program to get a feel for how close it is to processing correctly. At the end of the testing cycle when only minor changes are being made, the Zoom mode may be used to quickly find out if a specific change has brought about the anticipated result.

The Zoom mode of execution may be terminated by pressing the CTRL + BREAK keys. Otherwise, program execution will continue until either a STOP RUN COBOL statement is executed or a programmer-set Breakpoint is encountered. The Zoom mode is also often used in combination with the other execution modes through the use of Breakpoints (see below).

Using Breakpoints

A *Breakpoint* is a place in the program where it is desirable to pause the execution of a program being animated in either the Go or Zoom modes. Programmers set Breakpoints at places in the program where it is suspected there may be a problem or where it may be useful to observe the progress of processing results. Programmers often have a good idea which portions of their programs are most likely causing a problem. Therefore, it may be desirable to execute some portions of the program very rapidly using the Zoom or Go modes, but to stop in certain places and proceed in the Step mode. This may be accomplished by setting Breakpoints at the beginning of the areas where a pause is desired. For example, suppose a program is processing correctly except that one calculation is not being performed correctly. By setting a Breakpoint at the beginning of the module that performs the calculation, the programmer can use the Go or Zoom modes of animation to quickly execute the other modules and then switch to the Step mode to carefully analyze the calculation instructions.

Pressing the [B] key on the Animate Menu results in the display of the Breakpoints Menu illustrated in Figure 7.3. Place the cursor on the line of source code before which a pause is desired. Pressing the [S] key then sets a Breakpoint at this location and will cause a pause in the execution of the program each time this Breakpoint is encountered. Figure 7.4 illustrates how the Message Line appears after a Breakpoint has been encountered that was set on line 138 of the SAMPLE program.

Up to 100 Breakpoints may be set in a program. Existing Breakpoints may be located by using the Examine option. Each time the [E] key is pressed on the Breakpoints Menu, the cursor will move to the next line of source code containing a Breakpoint. All Breakpoints may be removed with the Breakpoint Menu Cancel-all option. *Also, all Breakpoints are automatically removed when a program is recompiled using Checker.* Individual Breakpoints may be removed with the Unset option on the Breakpoints Menu.

Monitoring Data Items during Animation

Another very useful feature of Animator is its ability to display the values contained in data items, either upon demand or continuously as the program executes. This gives the programmer the

```
122        MOVE 2                         TO REQD
123        PERFORM 211-PRINT-REPORT-LINE
124        MOVE COLUMN-HEADING-LINE       TO PRINT-AREA
125        MOVE 3                         TO REQD
126        PERFORM 211-PRINT-REPORT-LINE.
127
128 211-PRINT-REPORT-LINE.
129        WRITE PRINT-RECORD AFTER ADVANCING REQD LINES
130        ADD REQD                       TO LINE-COUNT.
131/
132 22-GET-INPUT-RECORD.
133        READ SAMPLE-DATA
134          AT END
135            MOVE "TRUE "              TO END-OF-FILE.
136
137 23-ACCUMULATE-TOTAL.
138        ADD IN-AMOUNT                  TO TOTAL-AMOUNT.
139
140 24-PRINT-DETAIL-LINE.
141        MOVE IN-NAME                   TO RPT-NAME
142        MOVE IN-AMOUNT                 TO RPT-AMOUNT
Break-points—On-count=unset————————————Level=01-Speed=5-Ins-Caps-Num-Scroll
F1=help F2=view F3=align F4=exchange F5=where F6=look-up  F9/F10=word-</> Escape
Set Unset Cancel-all Examine If Do On-count
```

Pressing the [S] key sets a Breakpoint at the line where the cursor is located.

Number of Breakpoints that have been set (currently, none are set).

Figure 7.3 *The Breakpoint Menu that appears when the [B] key is pressed on the Animate Menu.*

```
127
128 211-PRINT-REPORT-LINE.
129      WRITE PRINT-RECORD AFTER ADVANCING REQD LINES
130      ADD REQD                          TO LINE-COUNT.
131/
132 22-GET-INPUT-RECORD.
133      READ SAMPLE-DATA
134         AT END
135            MOVE "TRUE "                TO END-OF-FILE.
136
137 23-ACCUMULATE-TOTAL.
138      ADD IN-AMOUNT                     TO TOTAL-AMOUNT.
139
140 24-PRINT-DETAIL-LINE.
141      MOVE IN-NAME                      TO RPT-NAME
142      MOVE IN-AMOUNT                    TO RPT-AMOUNT
143      MOVE DETAIL-LINE                  TO PRINT-AREA
144      PERFORM 211-PRINT-REPORT-LINE
145      MOVE 2                            TO REQD.
146
147
Animate-SAMPLE----------------------------------Level=01-Speed=5-Ins-Caps-Num-Scroll
F1=help F2=view F3=align F4=exchange F5=where F6=look-up  F9/F10=word-</> Escape
Step Go Zoom next-If Perform Reset Break Env Query Find Locate Text Do 0-9=speed
```

Next instruction to be executed when Animator is reactivated.

Animator is reactivated after the pause by selecting one of these options.

Figure 7.4 *How the display appears when Animator encounters a Breakpoint that was set on line 138.*

opportunity to monitor changes in data values as processing progresses. This feature is very handy when output results are incorrect and the programmer is having difficulty determining the cause of the error.

Pressing the [Q] key on the Animate Menu results in the display of the Query Menu, as illustrated in Figure 7.5. There are two ways to identify the field of interest. Pressing the [E] key for Enter Name results in a prompt requesting entry of the COBOL source code identifier (name) of the

```
122      MOVE 2                            TO REQD
123      PERFORM 211-PRINT-REPORT-LINE
124      MOVE COLUMN-HEADING-LINE          TO PRINT-AREA
125      MOVE 3                            TO REQD
126      PERFORM 211-PRINT-REPORT-LINE.
127
128 211-PRINT-REPORT-LINE.
129      WRITE PRINT-RECORD AFTER ADVANCING REQD LINES
130      ADD REQD                          TO LINE-COUNT.
131/
132 22-GET-INPUT-RECORD.
133      READ SAMPLE-DATA
134         AT END
135            MOVE "TRUE "                TO END-OF-FILE.
136
137 23-ACCUMULATE-TOTAL.
138      ADD IN-AMOUNT                     TO TOTAL-AMOUNT.
139
140 24-PRINT-DETAIL-LINE.
141      MOVE IN-NAME                      TO RPT-NAME
142      MOVE IN-AMOUNT                    TO RPT-AMOUNT
Query-data--------------------------------------Level=01-Speed=5-Ins-Caps-Num-Scroll
F1=help F2=view F3=align F4=exchange F5=where F6=look-up  F9/F10=word-</> Escape
Cursor-name Enter-name Repeat Monitor-off Dump list
```

Place cursor here to query the value of TOTAL-AMOUNT.

Press [C] key to display value of the field where the cursor is located.

Figure 7.5 *Display appearing when the [Q] key is pressed on the Animate Menu.*

field. However, it is often easier to place the cursor under the field's name and press the [C] key for Cursor Name to identify the field of interest. Once either of these methods is accomplished, the display changes to show the name of the data item on the Information Line and the value currently stored in it on the Message Line. Figure 7.6 illustrates that the data item TOTAL-AMOUNT contains 000000+ (positive zero) when the SAMPLE program first begins to execute and before the first input data record has been fully processed. Any data item may be inspected during an execution pause. Using Breakpoints and/or the Step mode permits program execution to be suspended at any point in the program so that data item values may be seen. However, only one data item may be seen at a time.

```
Query:     TOTAL-AMOUNT──────────────Level=01-Speed=5-Ins-Caps-Num-Scroll
F1=help  F2=clear  F3=hex  F4=monitor                  ↑↓ =up/down data
F7=containing   F8=contained  F9=same level            ↵  Alt  Ctrl  Escape
000000+]
```

Current value is positive zero

Monitor option may be used to continuously display the value of the field during execution.

Figure 7.6 *The value contained in TOTAL-AMOUNT when program execution begins.*

Notice in the display shown in Figure 7.6 that there is a Monitor option that may be selected by pressing the [F4] key. This causes Animator to continuously display the value of a data item as the program executes so that changes in the value may be seen and associated with specific instructions in the source code. Figure 7.7 illustrates how the value of TOTAL-AMOUNT would appear just after the first input data record has been accumulated. The monitoring of a data item may be discontinued by pressing the [M] key on the Query Menu to select the Monitor-off option.

```
Monitor:  TOTAL-AMOUNT──────────────Level=02-Speed=5-Ins-Caps-Num-Scroll
F1=help  F2=view  F3=align  F4=exchange                                Escape
0-9=speed  Zoom
003616+]
```

Value after first input record was processed is positive 3616.

Figure 7.7 *How the Control Area appears during continuous monitoring of the TOTAL-AMOUNT field.*

Encountering Runtime Errors

There are many reasons why the execution of a program might terminate abnormally (often referred to as a program interrupt or abend). If the program instructs the computer to do something that it cannot, a runtime error is said to have occurred. When this happens, Animator terminates execution, displays an error message on the Message Line, and highlights the source code instruction that was being executed at the time of the error.

Two common reasons why program interrupts occur are because of file not found errors and data exception errors. Figure 7.8 illustrates what happened during the execution of the SAMPLE program when the filename in the ASSIGN clause for the input test data file was specified incorrectly. The computer could not find the specified filename in its directory when the instruction on line 100 was executed. Therefore it had to terminate execution of the program. A data exception error occurs when a data item specified as a numeric field is used in a calculation, comparison, or numeric editing instruction and, for some reason, does not actually contain a numeric value. The runtime error message displayed when this occurs is "Illegal character in numeric field (error 163)." This is usually caused by either an incorrect description of the input data record or the test file not being created with valid data.

```
 98
 99 12-OPEN-FILES.
100     OPEN INPUT  SAMPLE-DATA
101          OUTPUT SAMPLE-REPORT.
102
103
104
105 2-GET-AND-PROCESS-DATA.
106     IF LINE-COUNT > +53
107         PERFORM 21-PRINT-REPORT-HEADING
108         END-IF
109     PERFORM 22-GET-INPUT-RECORD
110     IF END-OF-FILE NOT = "TRUE "
111         PERFORM 23-ACCUMULATE-TOTAL
112         PERFORM 24-PRINT-DETAIL-LINE
113         END-IF.
114
115 21-PRINT-REPORT-HEADING.
116     MOVE TITLE-LINE              TO PRINT-AREA
117     WRITE PRINT-RECORD AFTER ADVANCING PAGE
118     MOVE +7                      TO LINE-COUNT
Animate-SAMPLE-------------------------Level=03-Speed=5-Ins-Caps-Num-Scroll
F1=help F2=view F3=align F4=exchange F5=where F6=look-up  F9/F10=word-</> Escape
Step Go Zoom next-If Perform Reset Break Env Query Find Locate Text Do 0-9=speed
File not found  (Error 013)
```

Instruction being executed when the run-time error occurred.

Runtime error message

Figure 7.8 *Typical display that appears when a runtime error occurs. In this example, the label of the test data file was not specified correctly in the ASSIGN clause so the file could not be opened.*

There are literally hundreds of possible runtime errors that can occur. Chapter 15 in the *Programmer's Guide* uses over 50 pages to describe the runtime errors identified by the Personal COBOL System. When a runtime error occurs, the error number displayed may be used to look up its corresponding description in the *Programmer's Guide*.

Exiting Animator

As with most other components of the Personal COBOL System, exiting Animator may be accomplished at any time by pressing the ESC key. The prompt "Exit from Animator? Y/N" is displayed. Pressing the Y key results in control being returned to Editor so that any required changes may be readily made to the source code of the program being tested.

Additional Features of Animator

Animator has many other useful features the description of which is beyond the scope of this manual. A full description of these features is available in Chapter 6 of the*Programmer's Guide*. Many of these features are better understood and used after some experience has been gained in testing programs. It is recommended that Chapter 6 of the*Programmer's Guide* be reviewed in its entirety periodically so that some familiarity with its other features is gained. Then, when a special situation is encountered when one of these features might be useful, the programmer is aware of it and can attempt to make use of it.

Chapter 8

Additional Features of Personal COBOL

Why Additional Features Are Needed

COBOL is a very versatile language that continues to evolve as processing requirements and programming techniques change. However, there is usually a significant time lag between when the need for a new language feature is recognized and when that feature is incorporated into the standard version of the language. As a leader in the evolution of the COBOL language, Micro Focus has attempted to solve this problem by including additional features and/or language extensions with its software development products to satisfy needs not yet accommodated by the standard language version.

Two areas that the current standard version, COBOL 85, does not handle well are applications requiring interactive user interfaces and certain operating system interactions. The Micro Focus Personal COBOL System includes some runtime support modules and COBOL language extensions that aid the programmer in dealing with these problems more efficiently. They include the SCREEN SECTION of the DATA DIVISION, a screen painting utility and code generator called Screens, and a runtime module called ADIS to support applications using advanced screen management features, function keys, and/or pointing devices such as a mouse. Also included is the Routines Library, a series of subprograms designed to be CALLed from a COBOL program for use in interacting with the operating system.

Screen Section

The SCREEN SECTION is a COBOL language extension designed to follow the WORKING-STORAGE SECTION of the DATA DIVISION. It may be used to describe areas of a display screen used for interactive applications like data entry and information display. One of its primary uses is for displaying a data entry form on the screen for the user to enter input data consisting of multiple fields. The SCREEN SECTION may also be used to display menus, messages, as well as output reports.

The standard COBOL language provides an ACCEPT statement, which may be used to retrieve a single data item entered via the keyboard. It also has a DISPLAY statement, which may be used to display one or more data items on the screen. However, these standard statements do not provide the ability to control the location or attributes of items appearing on the screen.

The SCREEN SECTION entries provide the ability for the programmer to describe large areas of the screen and specify their attributes. Each description entry in the SCREEN SECTION is referred to as a screen item or screen description. Screen item attributes might include field size, field position, editing, foreground color, background color, intensity, underlining, blinking, and/or reverse-video. Additional features are also available for cursor control, screen erasing, justification, default values, and security. The items described in the SCREEN SECTION are used by referencing them in ACCEPT and DISPLAY statements located in the PROCEDURE DIVISION. This greatly extends the usefulness of the ACCEPT and DISPLAY statements because the screen items referenced may be group items consisting of multiple entry/display fields, prompts, captions, headings, and/or messages each with their own attributes.

Many of the features provided through the use of SCREEN SECTION entries are also provided as language extensions of the ACCEPT and DISPLAY statements. They may be used directly as clauses included in any ACCEPT or DISPLAY statement.

Proper use of the SCREEN SECTION and the extensions to the ACCEPT and DISPLAY statements requires some experience in programming with COBOL. The COBOL syntax for the SCREEN SECTION as well as the ACCEPT and DISPLAY statement extensions may be found in Chapter 9 of the *Programmer's Guide*.

Screens

The Screens feature of the Personal COBOL System is a tool designed for use in quickly generating complex SCREEN SECTION entries. It is accessed by pressing the CTRL + F6 keys on the Editor Main Menu, followed by pressing the F7 key to select the Screens option.

The Screens feature allows a display screen to be "painted" on the screen. This is done by using the cursor control and editing keys to essentially draw a picture on the screen of how it is to appear when the program is executed. As the screen is painted, menu options may be selected to specify the attributes of the items placed on the screen. When the screen has been fully painted and all attributes specified, a code generator is invoked. The code generator uses the screen drawing and attribute specifications as input to produce a file containing a COBOL SCREEN SECTION entry. This file may then be included in a COBOL program during compilation by placing a COPY statement in the source code at the point where the generated code should appear.

This feature of Personal COBOL is not for the novice programmer. However, once some experience is gained in its use, the Screens feature is a very handy one. A complete description of Screens is included in Chapter 7 of the *Programmer's Guide*.

ADIS

ADIS is a runtime module that provides the necessary support during program execution to make use of the SCREEN SECTION and ACCEPT/DISPLAY language extensions. In addition, it may be used to support programs that make use of function keys and/or a mouse. It also provides the ability to alter screen and/or keyboard behaviors, either permanently by making changes to default settings or dynamically by making changes to settings as a program executes.

The proper use of ADIS is an advanced topic for experienced programmers. A description of ADIS features and its use is provided in Chapter 11 of the *Programmer's Guide*.

Library Routines

The library routines included in the runtime component of the Personal COBOL System supply capabilities not provided by COBOL syntax, such as operating system functions. The routines are used by including an appropriately phrased COBOL CALL statement in the PROCEDURE DIVISION. The CALL statement works similar to the PERFORM statement. Where the PERFORM statement executes the instructions in a paragraph internal to the program, the CALL statement executes the instructions in an external subprogram. The CALL statement may be used to exchange parameters and/or data between the calling program and the called subprogram.

The library routines supplied with Personal COBOL are described in Chapter 10 of the *Programmer's Guide.* They have been categorized by purpose for ease in locating their descriptions. These categories include Byte-Stream Files, Closedown Procedure, File-names, Files, Keyboard, Logic Operators, Mouse, Printer, Screen, and Text.

Some of the library routines provide similar capabilities to those supplied by the screen, keyboard, and mouse handling features associated with ADIS and the language extensions described earlier. However, there are several that may be useful for interacting with the operating system. For example, some of the routines in the Files category provide the ability to copy files, rename files, and access directory functions. There are also routines that may be used to change the case of text strings as well as routines to test the status of devices attached to the computer. The descriptions of these routines in the *Programmer's Guide* include all of the information necessary to determine what they do and how to invoke them. Again, the effective use of these routines requires some experience in programming with COBOL.

Appendix A

A Microcomputer Primer for Newcomers

An Overview of PC Hardware

In this section, we consider the most common components of a microcomputer, as known as a personal computer, PC, or "micro." We focus on the IBM family of personal computer. If you have an IBM-compatible machine you will find that your equipment is similar to the equipment shown in Figures A.1. Note that Micro Focus Personal COBOL is designed to run on IBM PC–equivalent compatible equipment. Personal COBOL will not run on Apple MacIntosh computers.

In the modern environment, most microcomputers are configured with these devices:

- Keyboard
- Monitor
- At least one hard disk drive and one or two floppies
- Printer
- Microprocessor (central processing unit)

We will examine each of these devices in the following sections of this appendix, beginning with the two varieties of keyboards commonly associated with IBM and IBM-compatible microcomputers.

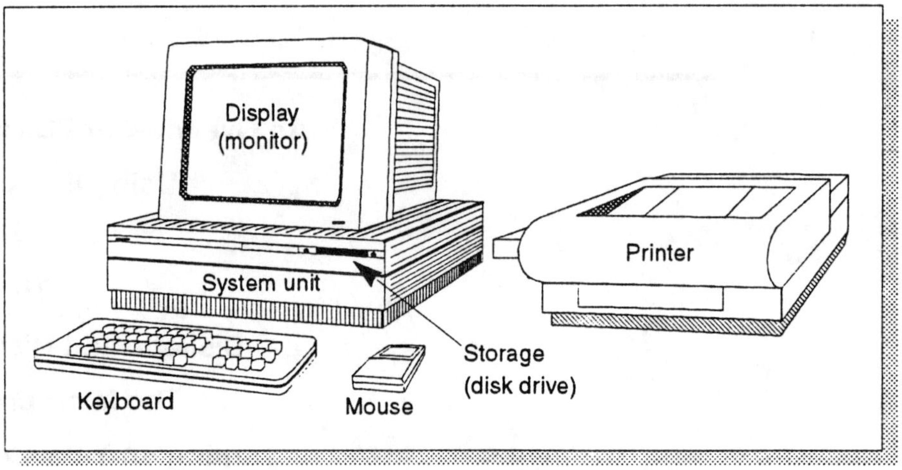

Figure A.1 *The IBM Personal System/2 Model 30*

Using the Keyboard

Keyboards are not always identical, but most keyboards include the basic keys in roughly the same positions. Figure A.2 illustrates the basic keyboard originated in 1981 with the first model of IBM PC, while Figure A.3 illustrates the enhanced keyboard introduced in 1987 by IBM. We provide a brief introduction to some of the more important keys on the keyboard.

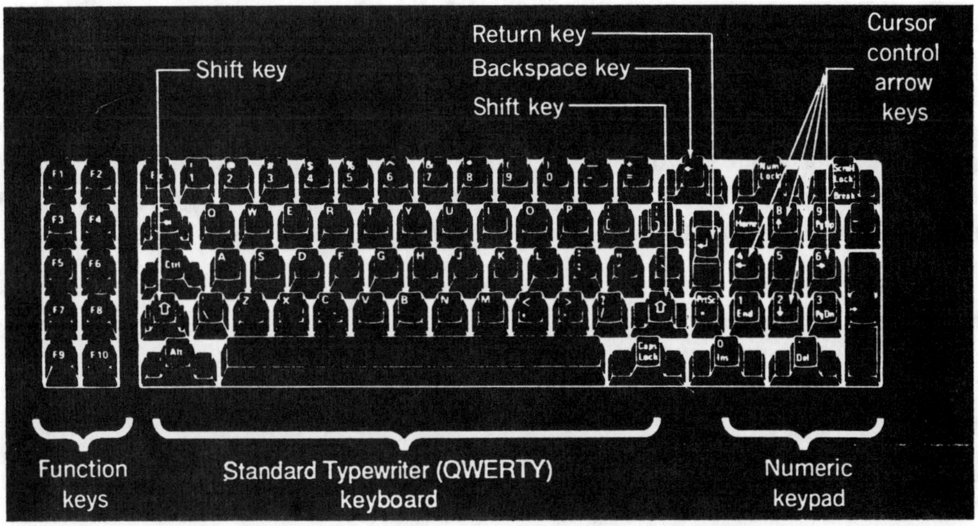

Figure A.2 *The Original IBM PC 83-key Keyboard (1981)*

Figure A.3 *The IBM PC 101-key Keyboard (1987)*

ENTER KEY

One of the most important keys on the keyboard is the Enter key. Keystrokes you make at the keyboard are received by the computer system and in most cases displayed on the screen and stored, but not acted upon, until you press . Enter might also be labeled Return. It is similar to a carriage return key on a typewriter. On an IBM PC the Enter key is marked with a leftward arrow (↵). Figure A.3 illustrates how this key appears on an enhanced keyboard, which labels it with both a leftward arrow and the word "Enter." In this guide, we will call this key the Enter key and it will be shown as [ENTER].

You type DOS commands and instructions and enter data using your keyboard as if it were a typewriter. When you are ready to send a line to the computer, press the Enter key. While data is received by the computer's screen handling software as you press each key, no data, instruction, or system command is transmitted to the computer for execution until you press Enter.

BACKSPACE KEY

You can make changes to an entry before pressing Enter by using the Backspace key. The Backspace key is usually marked with a straight left arrow (←); it's above the Enter key as shown in Figures A.2 and A.3. Each time you press Backspace the computer will delete one character to the left of your cursor point, and move the cursor one position leftward.

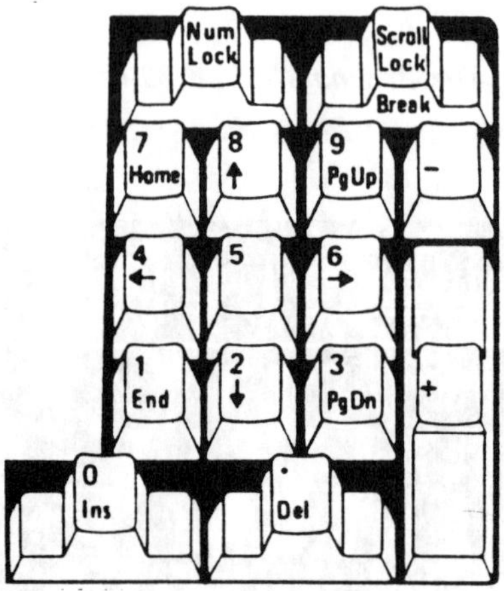

Figure A.4 *The Numeric Keypad*

NUMERIC KEYPAD

The numeric keypad is typically located at the right side of the keyboard and is shown in Figure A.4. The numeric keypad allows you to enter numbers with your right hand, without the need to use the numerals on the top row of the keyboard, when the [NUM LOCK] key is pressed. When NumLock is off, the 2, 4, 6,and 8 keys act as cursor movement keys.

[←] [→] [↑] [↓] CURSOR CONTROL KEYS

Cursor control keys such as [←], [→], [↑], [↓], [HOME], [END], [PG UP], and [PG DN] are used for positioning the cursor at a desired point on the screen. These either share the numeric keypad with numbers, as in Figure A.3, or may be on a separate dedicated group of keys, as in Figure A.4. Many programs use cursor arrow keys to highlight the commands you want to execute. You also use these keys for text editing when keying in or revising a program.

If there are cursor control characters on your numeric keypad, you can access them when NumLock is off. When the NumLock light is on, the keypad keys generate numbers rather than cursor control signals. You turn NumLock on and off by pressing the [NUM LOCK] key. How is NumLock set when your microcomputer starts operation? This varies with different machines. IBM PS/2s and some compatibles with enhanced keyboards will be in "number" mode initially and you must press the [NUM LOCK] key once to get into "cursor" mode.

[CAPS LOCK] CAPSLOCK KEY

The [CAPS LOCK] key is on the lower right side of the 83 key keyboard but is on the left side of the enhanced 101-key keyboard, as shown in Figures A.2 and A.3. CapsLock, like NumLock, is a toggle key. If you do not press it at all, lowercase letters are transmitted when the alphabetic keys are pressed. If you press the [CAPS LOCK] key once, each letter you subsequently enter will be transmitted as an uppercase letter. If you press the [CAPS LOCK] key again, you get lowercase letters again. A light usually appears on the keyboard if you have toggled CapsLock on. CapsLock affects only letters. It has no effect on the numbers and special symbols on the top line of the keyboard. For example, to transmit the asterisk (∗) above the number 8 on the top row of the keyboard, you must use the [SHIFT] key, which is marked with an upward-pointing arrow, even if the [CAPS LOCK] key is on.

We recommend that you enter your program using uppercase letters, with CapsLock on. Data files should also be entered using uppercase letters unless you are instructed to do otherwise. Note that if your program tests for an 'M' in a data field and you have entered a lowercase 'm', these characters will not be considered equal when the comparison is performed. This is one reason why using all uppercase letters for data may help you to avoid errors.

[SHIFT] SHIFT KEY

The [SHIFT] and [CAPS LOCK] keys function just as they do on a typewriter. To continuously enter data or instructions in uppercase mode press the [CAPS LOCK] key. To enter only some data or instructions in uppercase, and others in lowercase, use the [SHIFT] key to control the case. There are two identical [SHIFT] keys on the keyboards, one on the lower right side of the central keyboard and one on the lower left. The [SHIFT] keys make all the special characters above the numbers on the basic keyboard available. The [SHIFT] key is not a toggle key because it must be held down or pressed for each special character or uppercase letter desired. CapsLock, on the other hand, need only be pressed once to transmit all uppercase letters.

[PG UP] [PG DN] PAGEUP AND PAGEDOWN KEYS

When using the Micro Focus Personal COBOL text editor for entering program and data files and with many other types of text editors, the [PG DN] key on the numeric keypad will scroll, or move, one page (screen) down in a program or file. [PG UP] will scroll one page up in a program or file. If you press the CTRL key and the HOME key at the same time, the cursor will move to the beginning of the file. Pressing CTRL and END will bring the cursor to the end of a file.

F1 F10 FUNCTION KEYS

Function keys appear to the left of the main keyboard on the original 83-key keyboard, as shown in Figure A.2. On 101-key enhanced keyboards, function keys appear above the main keyboard, as shown in Figure A.3. Function keys are typically numbered F1 through F10 or F1 through F12. These keys have specific meanings for each software product that you run.

The Monitor

When you enter data using a keyboard, or when the computer responds to you, the keyed data and computer response are displayed on the monitor. Other names for the monitor are screen, cathode ray tube (CRT), and video display. Some monitors have a special "on" switch separate from the computer's on switch. If there is a switch or knob on the monitor marked "on/off", turn it on before getting started.

Older monitors are monochrome monitors, which means they are white and black, green and black, or amber and black. Most modern monitors provide color screens, which can display graphics as well as text. Monochrome monitors are adequate for use with Micro Focus Personal COBOL. We recommend, however, that you use a color monitor with the Editor to get the full benefit of its abilility to trace the execution of your programs, which it does using contrasting colors.

Monitors usually come with a knob for adjusting the screen's color and/or brightness. You can make adjustments to suit your tastes. Most monitors can display 25 lines of output and 80 characters per line.

The Printer

Printers are used to obtain a written or "hard" copy of programs, data, or output. All printers can print letters, digits, and special symbols in black ink but some can also print in color and can print graphics and characters as well.

Modern printers take the form of dot-matrix, ink jet, or laser printers. While many dot-matrix printers produce near-letter-quality output, ink jet and laser printers are faster, quieter, and produce higher-quality print. Most printers print 80 characters per line but some can print 100 to 120 characters per line as well. Printers are controlled by a power switch separate from the computer power switch.

Access to a printer is important for COBOL programming work on a microcomputer for several reasons. First, of course, you will want to be able to take a listing of your source code for a program away from the computer, to be able to study it, and, eventually, to be able to submit it for grading. Secondly, some of your programs will create reports as output, which are designed to be printed. But, at any point in your computer work, you might also want to obtain a printed copy of a screen display. To get a screen print with either DOS or Editor, press the SHIFT key on the left hand side of the keyboard and the PRTSC key on the right side of the keyboard. With PS/2 microcomputers and some compatibles, pressing PRTSC alone will produce a screen print.

Diskette and Disk Drives

In order to be run (executed), a program file (machine language) must first be loaded into the microprocessor. Similarly, data files to be processed into reports or updated must be available as machine readable input before they can be processed. These machine language and data files must be stored externally to memory, which is volatile and resumes a random bit pattern when power is removed. Disk storage is called *auxiliary storage* or *secondary storage* to distinguish it from the computer's memory, which is called *primary storage*. Bit patterns forming information remain in place on disk when the computer is turned off. We usually store data and programs as files on disks so that they can be used again without having to rekey them on the keyboard.

Microcomputers use two types of disks: floppy diskettes and hard disks. Floppy disks are called “floppy” because they use a thin, removable, flexible medium with a magnetic surface on which data is recorded. We use the term “floppy disk” and “diskette” interchangeably. “Hard” disks use rigid, non-removable aluminum plates coated with a magnetic surface, and are encased in a sealed unit.

Floppy disk-only systems typically use two floppy disk drives for auxiliary storage although computers with just a single floppy disk drive are available. But since the price of hard disk computer systems has fallen dramatically since 1990, floppy-only systems are obsolescent. In addition, floppy-only systems are much more awkward to use with modern software, which often requires frequent access to disk storage.

Hard disk systems typically have a hard disk and either one or two floppy disk drives. The most common type of diskette drive now is the 3-1/2 inch size. Many computer systems are configured with two diskette drives to facilitate copying and backup. Floppy disk drives are usually labeled A for the left or upper drive and B for the right or lower drive, if there is one. The hard drive is typically referred to as the C drive. Your system may also have hard drive designations of D, E, and so forth.

FLOPPY DISKETTES

Floppy disk drives may be built in as part of the microcomputer or they may be units housed in separate units from the computer. The photo in Figure A.1 shows in the floppy disk in an IBM PS/2 labeled as the “disk drive.” Floppy disks for most IBM PCs are 5¼ inch; newer computers, laptops, and notebook computers use 3½ inch diskettes, as shown in Figure A.5. Despite its size, a 3½ inch disk has a larger storage capacity than a 5¼ inch disk.

Standard double-sided double-density (DSDD) 5¼ inch disks can store approximately 360,000 bytes of data, while double-sided high-density diskettes (DSHD) can store about 1.2 megabytes (million bytes). While a high-density floppy diskette drive can read a standard (low) density diskette, a low-density diskette drive cannot read a high-density disk.

Double-sided double-density 3½ inch floppy diskettes are labeled 2DD and can store approximately 720,000 bytes, twice as much as 5¼ inch diskettes. High-density 3½ inch diskettes are labeled 2HD and can store 1.44 megabytes. As with 5¼ inch floppies, higher-density 3½ inch diskette drives can read and process both capacities of 3½ inch floppy, but lower-density diskette drives are limited to reading and writing lower-density diskettes. Technology has advanced and made it possible to store two to four megabytes on some special types of 3½ inch diskettes. As yet, neither diskettes for this purpose nor diskette drives to handle them are commonly used.

Figure A.5 *3½ Inch Floppies Are Replacing 5¼ Inch Floppies*

The smaller, 3½ inch disks have a number of advantages over the older 5¼ inch size. They have a hard plastic casing, rather than a thin flexible sleeve, and are more resistant to damage. In addition, 3½ inch disks have a metal cover over the magnetic media, which automatically slides away to reveal an opening to the disk when it is read or written. Whereas 5¼ inch disks use stick-on write protect tabs for write protection, which can fall off, each 3½ inch disk has a built-in plastic tab to prevent writing. Instead of attaching a gummed tape, you slide the tab to write protect the disk (the position closest to the edge is the write-protected position).

HARD DISKS

The hard disk is a much more versatile storage device than either 3½ inch or 5¼ inch floppy diskettes. A modern hard disk has a capacity of 40 to 320 or more megabytes. In addition to a much larger storage capacity than floppy diskettes, hard disks access data ten or more times as fast as floppy diskette.

Hard disks are used to permanently store both programs and data and eliminate the need to "swap" floppy disks in and out of diskette drives to process large programs or files. But hard disks are vulnerable to damage from mechanical or electrical shock. Do not move, carry, jar, or drop a microcomputer that has a hard disk when the machine is on. Unless the hard disk is shock-mounted and designed to accommodate movement during operation (as with many laptops) it can easily be damaged by such movement while it is running. Floppies are commonly used to make copies, or "back ups," of files and programs stored on hard disk, to preserve data in case of hard disk damage or failure.

HANDLING FLOPPY DISKS

Diskettes are relatively durable but they do not tolerate physical abuse very well. Always handle diskettes by their protective outer covering, taking care not to touch the metallic portion. Keep all diskettes away from magnetic fields such as those associated with televisions, telephones, microwaves, and other electrical devices. Do not bend 5¼ inch diskettes. Store diskettes in the envelopes that are supplied with them. Contrary to popular misconception, diskettes are not usually affected by the magnetic security scanning gates employed at airports, and we have not encountered problems with either floppies or hard disks in laptops in carry-on luggage that has been scanned.

Blank diskettes are provided with adhesive labels that you, yourself, attach to label them. Write on the label before you attach the label to the diskette. Use only a felt tip pen to mark on the label after it has been attached to the diskette.

To insert a disk in the A or B floppy disk drive, the drive door must be open. On some drives you must press a release to open it. Similarly, most drives must be closed before they can be used. A disk drive is active when the small light on its face is on. Do not insert a disk in a drive when the light is on because you could damage the mechanism that reads and writes data, and you might damage the diskette itself.

To protect a 5¼ inch diskette from being written on by accident, put an adhesive write-protect tab over the square notch on its right side. To protect a 3½ inch diskette from being written on by accident, slide the small plastic tab at its top to the position closest to the edge.

The Microprocessor

A microprocessor is the "brains" or processing unit of the system and performs all processing. It is referred to as the central processing unit (CPU). It is mounted on a circuit board inside the main unit, and consists of a chip that contains millions of integrated circuits, as shown in Figure A.6. The original IBM PCs of the early 1980s used the 8088 chip, manufactured by Intel Corporation. Modern PCs and compatibles use the faster 80386 and 80486 chips, or the Intel Pentium processor. (The Pentium was to be named the 80586 until Intel decided to use a name for it that could be trademarked. Numbers can't be registered as trademarks in the United States.)

The microprocessor stores data and processes all instructions. It uses two types of memory. Read-only memory (ROM) is electronic storage that is "prewired" to perform system functions. ROM is installed by the computer manufacturer and cannot be changed by the user. Random access memory (RAM) is changeable and stores programs and data loaded from external sources, such as floppy and hard disks.

On most microcomputers, the capacity of RAM is typically measured in megabytes (MB). A megabyte is approximately one million bytes. Two to sixteen megabytes of RAM is a common range for modern microcomputers.

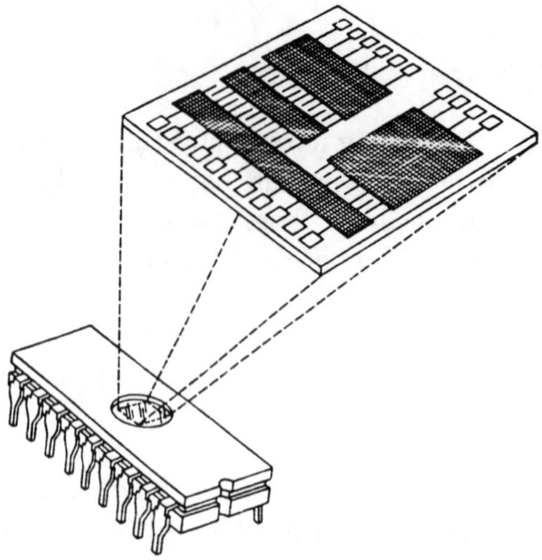

Figure A.6 *The Microprocessor "Chip" Contains Millions of Circuits*

Most modern software depends on access to several megabytes of RAM (memory) in your microcomputer, so one of the most important considerations you face when selecting a microcomputer is its memory capacity. A second consideration is hard disk capacity. We suggest that you acquire at least 80 to 100 megabytes or more of hard disk capacity in any microcomputer you buy. Thirdly, you should realize that much of the present generation of software is designed to run best on machines using 80486 chips. The 80386 chip is still popular, but earlier chips, such as the 80286, are not capable of supporting much modern software.

Turning on Your Computer

You will typically have several devices to turn on when you want to activate your computer. You should turn on your monitor and printer before turning on your computer. The power switches on these devices will vary in location, and you must become familiar with your own equipment complement.

Before actually turning on the microcomputer, determine whether or not you have a hard disk drive. For diskette systems with no hard drive, place a DOS operating diskette in the A drive before you turn on the computer. For computers with hard disks, the operating system is automatically loaded directly from the hard disk, and no diskette should be in any diskette drive. *Caution! One way that a destructive virus can enter a computer system is via an "infected" floppy that is present in a diskette drive when you turn on the power.* If a floppy is present, the microcomputer attempts to load the operating system from it before seeking this from the hard disk. On a system with a hard disk, *do not leave floppies in your diskettes drives when you turn on power.*

Most operating systems automatically perform a diagnostic hardware test to ensure that hardware components are working properly. If there is a hardware problem, you will be advised of it. If everything is okay, the computer will transmit a message and you will be given some form of prompt on the screen, which is a request for a user response.

Activating the DOS Operating System

Most modern microcomputers have an internal clock that automatically keeps track of the date and time. If yours has one, your system is probably configured to omit any request to you to enter the date and time. In this case you will receive a prompt that looks like:

`C:>` *(for hard disk systems)*

This means that the computer is ready for you to begin work. Whenever an **A:>** or **C:>** prompt appears, whatever you type in will be processed by the DOS operating system. Starting up the computer in this way is referred to as "booting" the system. If you arrive automatically at this prompt, you may bypass the following discussion, and skip to *Rebooting or Restarting the Computer* below.

If your computer system does not have an internal clock, you will most likely be asked to supply the date and time with this prompt:

```
Current date is Tuesday 1-01-1980
Enter new date:     [   ]
```

The form of the date entry is **MM-DD-YY**, where **MM** is a two-digit month, **DD** is a two-digit day, and **YY** is a two-digit year. Thus you would enter **05-27-94** for May 27, 1994. If the system prompts you to enter a new time you may enter the time as **HH:MM.SS** where **HH** is hours, **MM** is minutes, and **SS** is seconds (optional). DOS assumes a 24-hour clock. 1:00 A.M. to noon is 01 to 12, and 1:00 P.M. becomes 13, 2 P.M. is 14, and so on. For example, you can enter 1:06 P.M. as 13:06. Remember to press the ENTER key after entering the date and also after the time has been entered. The DOS message displayed following the date and time may vary, depending on your computer and the version of DOS you are using.

You can ignore the DOS request for date and time by pressing the ENTER key when "Enter new date:" and "Enter new time:" are displayed. It is, however, useful to make these entries because the date and time will be recorded for each program you create or change. In this way, your directory of programs will include the date and time each was created or changed. This can also help distinguish between copies of programs that you have created earlier that are now obsolete.

Rebooting or Restarting the Computer

Restarting your computer after it has been turned on and booted up is called "rebooting." This is necessary only if a software you are executing fails and "locks up" (freezes) the system, making it impossible for you to control the machine. To reboot, you press the CTRL, ALT and DEL keys together. Some computers have a reset switch or button that functions like CTRL + ALT + DEL.

You can always restart your computer by turning the machine off, waiting a few seconds, and then turning the computer back on again. For diskette systems, make certain that your operating system is in the A drive. For hard disk systems, make sure there is no diskette in the A drive (the hard disk already contains the operating system). Restarting a computer by turning it off and on again is called a *cold start* as opposed to pressing [CTRL], [ALT] and [DEL], which is called a *warm start*. Cold starts take longer because you must wait a few seconds before turning the machine on again, and more hardware tests need to be performed during booting.

Summary of DOS Commands

You enter DOS operating system commands at the **C:>** prompt to cause the microcomputer to take specific actions. Listed below is a summary of the most common DOS commands. In this listing, [ENTER] means that you press the Enter or Return key, and **FILENAME.EXT** means the name of the file you want to manipulate. The file name may be up to eight characters, followed by a period, and this followed by an "extension" of the name of up to three characters. Source code files for the Micro Focus Personal COBOL compiler should be named with up to eight characters, followed by a period, followed by the letters CBL. The compiler creates object files using the source code file name followed by the extension .COB.

C:> DIR

Lists all of the files in the current directory, as well as their size in bytes and the date and time each was last changed. The file names will be roughly in the order in which you created the files. An exception occurs when you have erased any files, and later created new ones. You will see some of the newer file names occupying the same place in the listing of file names as was previously occupied by an erased file. To see the list of file names in the directory in sorted sequence, use the command:

```
C:> dir | sort [ENTER]
```

You can use the asterisk symbol (*) as a "wild card" to form filters to access only certain files in a directory listing or copy command. The * takes the place of any other one or more characters. For example, the command

```
C:> dir *.cbl [ENTER]
```

will list the names of any files that end with the file name extension .CBL. The command

```
C:> dir test1.* [ENTER]
```

will list the names of any files that have TEST1 as the file name and any extension.

If the subdirectory in which you are working contains more than about 20 file names, you will want to use the directory command followed by **/p**, such as:

```
C:> dir /p [ENTER]
```

The **/p** tells the system to pause after showing a full screen ("page") of the directory. You can see the next screen by pressing the [ENTER] key.

C:> TYPE *FILENAME.EXT*

Shows the contents of the file named filename.ext. Note that the system will direct this to the screen very quickly, and if the file has more than a few hundred bytes in it, the beginning will quickly scroll off the screen. To pause at each full screen of a file you are displaying on the screen, use the type command with a pipe to the MORE function:

```
C:> type FILENAME.EXT ¦ more [ENTER]
```

C:> COPY *FILENAME1.EXT FILENAME2.EXT*

Copies the first file named to a new file. If the file named atFILENAME2.EXT already exists, it is overwritten but you are given a warning message or chance to cancel the copy action.

C:> RENAME *FILENAME1.EXT FILENAME2.EXT*

Change the name of the file named filename1.ext to the name FILENAME2.EXT. If FILENAME1.EXT does not exist, or FILENAME2.EXT already exists, an error message is produced.

C:> ERASE *FILENAME.EXT*

Eliminates filename.ext from the directory. The file remains on disk, but cannot be accessed. Some types of utility programs give you the ability to "unerase" a file erased by mistake, but only if you have caused no other disk activity since the erasure.

C:> CD*DIRNAME*

Changes the "current" directory to the name specified. If you have executed the directive `prompt $p$g` either at the keyboard or by placing it into your AUTOEXEC.BAT file, you will see the directory in which you are active at the prompt. Directories are used to group and organize information instead of having all files housed in one large heap.

The directory indicated by just the backslash (\) with no name is the "root directory." It should contain only a few important system files and the names of all of the other directories on the system. Technically, all directories but the root directory are known as subdirectories.

C:> MD *SUBDIR*

Creates a subdirectory named subdir. Subdirectory names can be up to eight characters long. The subdirectory is housed within the directory in which you are "current" when you take this action.

C:> RD *SUBDIR*

Eliminates a subdirectory if it is empty (contains no files), otherwise an error message is issued. In order to eliminate a subdirectory you have to:

- Erase all of the files within the subdirectory
- Be within the directory in which it is housed and issue the **RD** command.

Using an AUTOEXEC.BAT File

AUTOEXEC.BAT is a special file name. If a file of this name is contained in the root directory, DOS reads it and executes any commands in it as a part of the system startup process. You can create and put commands into AUTOEXEC.BAT using any text editor capable of creating ASCII files. You can use the Personal COBOL Editor to do this.

One handy command that you should put into your AUTOEXEC.BAT file is:

```
prompt p$g$
```

This command tells DOS to display the name of the directory and subdirectory in which you are current, as a part of the normal system prompt. For example, if the **`prompt p$g$`** command has been invoked, and you are in the MFCOBOL subdirectory, the prompt will look like this:

```
C:\MFCOBOL>
```

Micro Focus Personal COBOL does not require any special system setup or features in order for you to use it. But your Personal COBOL files are housed in the subdirectory named MFCOBOL if you used the installation procedure described on page 8 in Chapter 2 of this guide. When you installed Micro Focus Personal COBOL, you were asked in step 10 of the installation process about changing your AUTOEXEC.BAT file.

If you do not use an AUTOEXEC.BAT file, the system will prompt you for the entry of date and time. To eliminate these prompts create an AUTOEXEC.BAT file and put at least this command into it:

```
ECHO OFF
```

Deactivating the NumLock Key

Some computer systems such as the IBM PS/2 start up as if the [NUM LOCK] key had been pressed, to make the numeric keypad ready for the entry of numbers in a "data entry" mode. On such a machine, the "NumLock" light will be on when you start the computer system. Press [NUM LOCK] once to shut off the NumLock light and make the numeric keypad arrow keys work as you expect them to.

Self Test

Assess your comprehension of basic microcomputer knowledge by taking this self test. The correct answer to each question is provided on the next page.

1. "Micro" is an abbreviation for ______________________.

2. Another term used to describe a "micro" is ______________________.

3. The main hard disk drive of a micro is typically called the ________________ drive.

4. Before turning on a microcomputer, you should have a ____________ diskette in the main drive unless you have a hard disk.

5. (T or F) There are usually two sets of keys on a keyboard that can be used for entering numbers.

6. Before data is transmitted to a program, the ______________ key must be depressed.

7. The most common operating system for an IBM microcomputer is called ____________.

8. DOS begins by asking for the ____________ and the ______________ unless you have an ______________ ______________.

9. The danger posed by leaving a diskette in a microcomputer with a hard disk when you turn on (boot up) the system is that a ________________ may enter the system from an infected diskette.

10. Disk storage is also called ______________ storage or __________ storage.

11. RAM stands for ______________ ______________ ______________.

12. You write-protect a 3½ inch floppy diskette by moving the write protect tab to the __________________ edge.

13. ROM stands for ______________ ______________ ______________ and is not alterable by a computer user.

14. When you start using your computer, you should turn on your ______________ and ______________ first, then your ______________.

15. Turning off the power to a computer, waiting a few seconds, and turning it on again is known as a ______________ start.

16. (T or F) When you copy one file to another using the DOS COPY command, and the file you are copying to already exists, you do not get a warning message but the existing file is overwritten.

Solutions To Self Test

1. microcomputer
2. personal computer
3. C
4. DOS
5. T (true); the top row of the main keyboard and the numeric keypad can both be used to enter numbers.
6. Enter or Return
7. DOS
8. date, time; internal clock
9. virus
10. auxiliary, secondary
11. random access memory
12. outer
13. read only memory
14. monitor, printer, computer
15. cold
16. T (true); `COPY` replaces an existing file with the one you indicated should be copied to it.

Index